He She
WINS WINS

**Dr. Glenn P.
ZAEPFEL**

OLIVER
NELSON

THOMAS NELSON PUBLISHERS
Nashville

Published in Nashville, Tennessee, by Thomas Nelson, Inc., Publishers, and distributed in Canada by Word Communications, Ltd., Richmond, British Columbia.

The Bible version used in this publication is the HOLY BIBLE, NEW INTERNA-TIONAL VERSION®. Copyright © 1973, 1978, 1984 by International Bible Society. Used by permission of Zondervan Publishing House. All rights reserved. Scripture quotations noted NKJV are from THE NEW KING JAMES VERSION. Copyright © 1979, 1980, 1982, Thomas Nelson, Inc., Publishers. Scripture quotations noted NASB are from the New American Standard Bible, © 1960, 1962, 1963, 1968, 1971, 1972, 1973, 1975, 1977 by The Lockman Foundation. Used by permission. Scripture quotations noted AMPLIFIED are from THE AMPLIFIED BIBLE: Old Testament. Copyright © 1962, 1964 by Zondervan Publishing House (used by permission); and from THE AMPLIFIED NEW TESTAMENT. Copyright © 1958 by The Lockman Foundation (used by permission).

ISBN 0-8407-9206-9

Printed in the United States of America.

This book is respectfully and lovingly dedicated to three influential men, all of whom were called home early to be with our Lord during 1991:

Walter Zaepfel—*my loving and giving father who taught me of laughter, faithfulness, commitment, selflessness, and responsibility*

Lee Atwater—*a brilliant political mind and my dear old pal who taught the world of politics, the blessings of family and loving friendships, the fun of music, the value of repentance, the importance of faith, and the centrality of Christ in the short lives we are given*

Dr. William Crabb—*my encouraging and inspiring colleague who taught Christ's psychology and the life-style of the living and of the dead*

They are missed greatly.

[**zaepfel**—zep´fǝl—zepfle—zep´ful]

CONTENTS

ACKNOWLEDGMENTS

I am very grateful to a number of folks who gave me helpful feedback in the preparation of this manuscript—particularly John and Denise Thomas who painstakingly combed through, and helped groom, the text. I am also indebted to Steve and Jane Simmons, George and Cathy Crow, Joe and Barbara Novenson, Michael and Susan Sexton, Dr. Darrell Shaver, Diane Morrison, and Bob Yount (Buffalo Bob who, thanks to the Lord, is still on the planet). But the individuals who mattered the most were in my very own family. Linda helped considerably with her on-the-spot editing, insights, clarifying comments, typing abilities, emotional support, encouragement, and prayers. Peter, Carrie, and Christine constantly bathed this work in prayer and patiently and lovingly gave up some "Dad time" to allow the manuscript to get finished. I must also acknowledge my appreciation and respect for a host of clients, who in the therapy process came to be dear friends, for sharing and entrusting their lives and problems with me, which simultaneously taught me about the realties of the power-passive dynamic. Above all, thanks and praises go to the Lord Jesus Christ who gave me the contents, time, resources, abilities, and energies to get this work out.

INTRODUCTION

This book is addressed to two groups of individuals, within the framework of marriage, who don't know how to live a balanced Christian life, and who may be enduring much needless suffering due to relationships that, knowingly or unknowingly, abuse them emotionally. The first group of individuals is on the extreme end of a continuum of personal care: they neglect themselves too much. For such individuals, such things as passivity, dependency, tolerance of forms of abuse, and poor self-esteem are important personality and/or relational components.

The second group of individuals is on the opposite end of that same continuum of personal care. These individuals may believe that they are more balanced than they really are. Though their heads are in the right place, their hearts often miss the mark. They try intensely and earnestly to do the right thing and to meet all the right requirements of life. In fact, these individuals are often successful in other areas of life, such as in business, but these same winning attributes don't work in intimate relationships. These individuals lack the ability to give of themselves in an appropriately caring manner to others because their world is constructed to provide false feelings of power and control. For these individuals, such things as order, structure, rules, authority, legalism, and procedure are the glue that holds their world together. As with the first group of people, there is a range for this group. This second group, knowingly or unknowingly, hurts the first group. Both groups also injure the church.

There is a basic distinction between the individual who practices discipline and purity and the individual who practices the counterfeits of power and rigidity. The former represents a pattern of spiritual victory while the latter constitutes a pattern of psychological egotism and failure. Likewise, there is a similar distinction between the person who practices biblical behaviors, such as submission, and the person who practices passive-dependency. The former indicates a pattern of spiritual compliance and triumph while the latter suggests a pattern of psychological selfishness and defeat.

The emphasis of this book is on the marital relationship and on the power partner and the passive partner who stand at unbalanced, opposite ends of the relational continuum. It clarifies how marital roles are undermined by unrecognized, subtle, and destructive psychological and spiritual processes. The first kind of person and the second kind of person need each other. Unknowingly, they feed off each other until the damage becomes so unbearable that one or both parties become severely injured emotionally. The hope of this book is to prevent such damage before it gets to that point. For those couples where it has already reached that point, the hope is to prevent destruction of the individuals and/or the relationship.

The terms used here to describe the power and passive continuums of behavior (e.g., *power*, *rigid*, *passive*, and *satisfier*) denote the controlling and legalistic versus passive-dependent individuals described above. These terms are used in a spirited, affectionate, animated, yet respectful manner. The idea is to depict two broad ranges of behaviors (and continuums for each) while indicating a degree of distaste for them. A psychological principle—referred to as aversive counterconditioning—explains that a mildly distasteful term can be effective in reducing behaviors attributed to that term.

We don't like to think of ourselves as *power persons*, *rigid persons*, *passive persons*, or *satisfiers*. Yet if we're honest, we can see the usefulness of such names to denote behaviors appropriate to the implementation of these terms. If it looks like a duck, walks like a duck, and quacks like a duck, it probably is a duck. If after understanding the definitions of these terms as used in this book, anyone notices that such descriptors may apply to personal behaviors, that individual can no longer ''duck'' the issue.

The book also explains how, through unconscious processes, these two groups become confusedly and destructively intertwined. *Such unconscious relational processes may occur only in certain relationships, such as the marriage relationship, and the characteristics of each personality type may be confined to that one relationship.* An individual may not be a complete passive person or power person but a pseudopassive or pseudopower, confining such qualities and behaviors to only one relationship or setting. The book focuses on the power and passive roles in the marital relationship. Such power and passive roles and behaviors are subtle but dangerous perversions of biblical marriage and behaviors. It is also true that a power person in one relationship may be a passive partner in another (and vice versa). For example, a power husband may be a passive person in certain business or professional relationships. A passive wife may be a power person with her kids, friends, work peers, or relatives. People who know the couple may not at all fully recognize these deeper processes and can easily be fooled because these marital dynamics occur silently and behind closed doors.

Such unconscious processes may be compared to the composing of music by two composers who somehow become attracted to each other's musical abilities. From the earliest days of each composer's family life, a mysterious melody was being composed in the life of its children. Though it affected each member somewhat differently, the melody was embellished by other traits and influences and became uniquely musical in the life of each particular child.

Later in life, both children unconsciously cultivated that melody to be a part of their very emotional essence. It was not something the individual was aware of, yet it was as much a part of the person as the inner being. In the search for a potential mate, that unconscious melody, above everything else, would determine who would become the person's mate.

Simply stated, the melody maker would search for the perfect lyricist to complete the harmonious union. The melody maker would be attracted to the individual whose developmental process allowed the perfect blending of meter, rhythm, tone, pitch, and timbre to allow the musical composition to begin to flow and to take on direction. In the excitement of the attraction process and of the first strains of musical symmetry that seemed to be finally working, neither member was aware that the song that had begun would become a death march.

The hope of this book is that Christ will orchestrate a new song in the individual, relational, and corporal symphony of the power-passive dynamic. It is the intention to create an awareness of the processes involved in the orchestration of the power-passive dirge. It is the hope that such awareness will lead to change; to individual, relational, family, and corporal healing; and to conformity to Christ's image and His direction for each of us. Psalm 40:3 clarifies this hope:

> He put a new song in my mouth,
>   a hymn of praise to our God.
> Many will see and fear
>   and put their trust in the LORD.

All of the stories used in this book reflect my work with clients. Information is disguised to provide protection and confidentiality for clients and the actual situations. Names used are purely fictional and often descriptive (e.g., "Debbie Dent" is a derivative of "dependent"; "Ron Rodman" is used to denote "a man who is like a rod").

Chapter 1

THE POWER PARTNER

Just as his wife, Patsy, had expected, Ron Rodman seemed uncomfortable in my counseling office. Ron was a respected leader in his church who provided counseling for church members. Patsy had come to see me only weeks earlier feeling intensely depressed with suicidal thoughts. She had tried very hard to be the best biblical wife she could be, yet she felt burned out, lethargic, lifeless, and drained. Patsy would need a few more sessions to realize the underlying intense anger and resentment she harbored. When she did, she denied herself the right to even have such feelings. She repressed them and converted them into worse depression. As if that wasn't bad enough, Patsy felt ashamed and humiliated that, despite her earnest efforts at being the best wife she could be by her biblical understanding of the wife's role, she had failed her husband, her family, her congregation, herself, and her Lord.

Ron pessimistically explained that they had been through counseling before, and that he didn't think this particular time would be any different. According to Ron, the problem was always the same: Patsy needed to let go of the past and be obedient to the Word. If she could just do that, their marriage would be okay again. The problem was that she wouldn't do it, and her lack of response was disobedience.

When I asked about their previous therapy, Ron unhesitatingly stated that their counseling had been done in his church. When I asked who did the counseling, Ron explained that he was the counselor. The problem was, again, that Patsy wouldn't follow his instructions so that constituted disobedience not only to her husband but also to her counselor and her church!

All my graduate training and clinical supervision hadn't adequately prepared me for such a moment. I thought I must have missed something or misheard what Ron said. But he actually had Patsy come into the church office, and he preached Ephesians 5:21 at her, admonishing her to be submissive to him in the dual role of husband and counselor. Patsy tried to do as he asked, yet her symptoms of depression seemed to continually worsen.

Ron instructed Patsy in submissiveness, obedience, what to do and how to do it, and why Scripture said what it said to her. But he made a few unintentional mistakes in his fervor to "fix" her: he was going by the letter of the law rather than by the spirit of the law, and he completely discounted Patsy's feelings. Her feelings were unimportant compared to what Ron believed to be scriptural directives.

Respect your feelings.

Of course, in some instances feelings ought to be ignored when they get in the way of following God's Word. That does not mean, however, that feelings should be dismissed entirely. Rather, they should be appropriately respected as we follow God in obedience. It didn't hurt matters, as far as Ron was concerned, that Scripture supported his views (whether or not it actually did). For him, the important issue was that he was right and Patsy needed to comply. It was God's design, and his role was to enforce it. Patsy shouldn't question Ron's guidance; she should submissively comply.

Mistaken Understanding of Submission

The fact that Ron had tried to enforce Ephesians 5:22 ("Wives, submit to your husbands as to the Lord") and gloss over Ephesians 5:21 ("Submit to one another out of reverence for Christ") suggested he was more interested in the letter of the law and missed the spirit of the law. Scripture was expositing not the virtues of Patsy's doing whatever Ron wanted but the principle of mutual submission, which goes against what Ron's behavior was communicating to her. By that interpretation of Scripture, Patsy really did count, and her feelings were to be respected. Feelings are not to run our lives, but we must care for others and what's going on inside them. We need to learn to be more sensitive to how our communication affects others than to what we are trying to communicate. For the power partner, it's more a matter of what the law apparently dictates than it is a matter of how the person is being affected by what's going on. Ron showed characteristics of the power partner.

Ron never really heard the pain Patsy was trying to communicate. He focused on doing what he thought was most appropriate: following God's directives. He was unaware that he was filtering such directives through the grid of his needs and motivation. Scripture tells us that "where there is no counsel, the people fall; but in the multitude of counselors there is safety" (Prov. 11:14 NKJV). Nevertheless, Ron felt his handling of the matter was sufficient, even in the face of Patsy's obvious discontent. He chose a scriptural passage that was more advantageous to his position (see Eph. 5:22) while ignoring other passages that were necessary to an appropriate understanding of his actual responsibility (see Prov. 11:14; Eph. 5:21).

Sound Christian guidance would have challenged Ron's narrow position in the context of God's greater and broader counsel. Christians cannot pick and choose what Scriptures suit our personal purposes. Rather, we must make our purposes align with the whole counsel of God's Word. Power partners specifically tailor their world, including how they perceive God's leading, to suit another plan: their unconscious agenda around their needs.

This process is unconscious, which means it is below persons' awareness of what is going on. What confounds and confuses the matter all the more is that such persons may be on target in other spiritual things, especially in the area of right versus wrong. But such individuals, though they preached a great sermon, led an insightful Bible study, or wrote a helpful book, may continue right along with being power partners. Others experience the effects of their influence and rigidity but can't quite tie things together because, in some ways, the power partners seem right. Perhaps nothing is more deceptive than partial truth.

Patsy compliantly went along with whatever Ron said. Power partners are adept at making others feel inferior, inadequate, or confused as a means of having their own way. After all, Ron was the one with all the training. Besides, he had shown her exactly where Scripture supported his views. Additionally, Ron's position paralleled Patsy's understanding of the situation from a Christian perspective.

Power Reversals

Patsy showed a few characteristics of the power partner. Passive partners can become power persons in other relationships, and power persons can become passive! This reversal applies to all power and passive-dependent individuals, but it especially applies to relational power-passivity. Relational power-passivity refers to the situation where the relationship itself creates power and follower roles. Some power-passive personality types are fairly consistent with characterological functioning across various relationships. Both versions of power-passivity are equivalent in form, though they differ in terms of substance. This working understanding becomes more complicated when we consider that there can also be a combination of these two versions of power-passivity.

Patsy showed core characteristics of the passive partner. She demurred without question to all of Ron's contentions, even at times when his leadership conflicted with God's intentions. Not all passive partners are found in these relationships, but it is amazing how many passive partners get hooked up with power partners. By her passivity, Patsy gave silent assent to Ron's rigidity; subsequently, she became rigid, also.

In Patsy's case, the rigidity was passive. She knew something didn't seem right, but it wasn't her place to question their relationship. I do not at all mean question in the defiant, disrespectful sense. Eventually going for counseling was a bold and crowning step for her. It was done with reluctant consent by Ron, who unconsciously punished her for seeking outside help. Yet Patsy realized at some questioning level within her that God's real plan for their relationship, as well as for Patsy as a woman, wife, and mother, seemed to be in jeopardy. At the very least, good Christian counsel could help her sort out all the mixed feelings inside her and thereby conform to God's purposes in a fuller way.

Patsy had reported long ago losing the joy of her salvation as well as the happiness in her home. She mechanically and ritually went through the tasks of everyday living, but something inside was dying. She felt angry about it but then guilty about feeling angry. After all, many people looked to her as a role model for victorious Christian living. What right did she have to feel so lousy?

Ron was dogmatic in his approach to their problems. He resented outside counseling unless it was counsel to back him up by telling Patsy to shape up and do what he said. Ron also felt quite authoritative. He had studied God's Word and really didn't need someone else telling him what to do. To Ron, Patsy was clearly wrong. He saw most of life through black-and-white spectacles. He was suspicious of those who didn't see life the way he did. He viewed such people as dangerous.

Ron was also uncompromising. He hardly ever budged on a stand. Again, such strong conviction can seem right in certain contexts, especially relating to Christian morals, values, and teaching. In some of these areas, it can be very right indeed. But for the power partner, such strong beliefs apply to almost all situations. The ability to be appropriately flexible is lacking or begrudgingly tolerated.

Ron was more interested in being right about Patsy's problem than in being open to how much more might be involved— especially in considering that he might be part of the problem! Ron came to counseling only once and then, shortly thereafter, made an executive decision for Patsy that she need not continue.

Unfortunate but Predictable

Months later I received a phone call from Patsy explaining she had opted to leave Ron and the church. Patsy clarified that counseling was helpful and she very much appreciated the unconditional love she felt there. She wished that she could have continued, but Ron made her feel that, in the bigger picture of their continuing relationship, she needed to do just what he desired. Despite my pleas to the contrary, Patsy decided to start a new life with another man who had shown her tolerance, kindness, and compassion, even though he was not a believer. He made her feel special, as if she really did matter to him. She felt the only other option for her was continued depression and discouragement, and she bailed out before taking her own life. Outwardly, she looked like the bad guy of the relationship. What she did was clearly wrong but emotionally predictable.

Power Is Not Easy to See

Ron possessed obvious traits of the power partner. However, it's not always so easy to detect power partners even when they may be right under our noses. Sometimes they can be found in leadership situations where they are less readily detectable.

Their influence is felt, but it's hard to trace the impact back directly to them. Sometimes they are parents; sometimes they are employers or supervisors; sometimes they are ministers, counselors, or authors. If you really want to identify power personalities, look for passive partners. Power partners will find ways to try to influence or subjugate passive partners.

It's not always easy to find passive partners, either. They have just as many disguises as power partners. In fact, passive partners use some of the very same facades. But passive partners won't fight as much; once you've spotted them, the battle is all but over.

In many workable relationships, one person is a strong, disciplined, loving, caring, nurturing, and serving leader, and the other person is a submissive, giving, loving, nurturing follower, who is also capable of leading. Such a relationship should not be confused with the power-passive relationship. It is biblical and healthy. The power-passive relationship is not.

Rx for Healing

But be careful! This book should come with a warning from the surgeon general's office that states, "Caution: reading this book can be hazardous to your mental health. Not reading it, however, can be lethal." For those who persevere, freedom and healing are ahead. But there is no way to escape the emotional pain. My prayer is that you are ready to deal with the pain and fear now, before the cancerous effects go too far and cost too much. You've already paid too high a price. Christ will help you. His death on the cross opened the way for your new life. But healing is not just a matter of intensifying your faith or shaping up your walk. There's a lot of work to get done; there's a process to undergo; there's a transformation to experience.

But even persons with cancer can deny their diagnosis. They simply can't accept it so they psychologically look the other way. Avoidance can occur for the passive partner or the power partner as well. I encourage you to honestly examine yourself and your life situation.

Denying the Not So Obvious

A physician discovered a tumor in my left ankle about eighteen years ago. When he showed me the X ray and explained the situation to me, I remember very coherently asking him if he noticed that the room seemed to be tilting. I was also quick to discover that everything seemed to be getting very clouded. He escorted me back to the examining table and helped me lie down. I hadn't noticed how very close the ceiling was before.

Christ will help you heal.

In that situation, I was fading fast. If I could have gotten out of there, I would have, but he had my shoe and sock, and the room wouldn't straighten up. I didn't want to face or accept the reality of my situation. The word *tumor* sent shivers up my psyche. If I could have just gotten out of there, I could have convinced myself he really said "toe mar" or "two Ma's" or "two more" or "allergic reaction."

Marginal power partners may consider they might possess some power characteristics and be willing to work on change. But even moderate power partners will deny any problem to the hilt. They do not want to hear such things because they know what I knew when the doctor told me "tumor": something has to be done; it can't stay like this. One unwritten rule for both the power partner and the passive partner is, "It will stay like this; don't rock the boat; don't change anything." Sacrificers may recognize the problem but be afraid of doing anything about it. But not doing anything about it is, in fact, doing something about it. It is passively accepting defeat and possible death. I entered the hospital the next day. The rooms didn't tilt or fade.

is no such thing as a biblical power Christian or a biblical power partner as used in this book. The very opposite is true. Christians are strengthened by the recognition of their weakness and subsequent dependence on Christ alone. This plain and simple truth is one of the great paradoxes and freedoms of Christianity. It is what the apostle Paul meant when he wrote, ''But he said to me, 'My grace is sufficient for you, for my power is made perfect in weakness.' Therefore I will boast all the more gladly about my weaknesses, so that Christ's power may rest on me. That is why, for Christ's sake, I delight in weaknesses, in insults, in hardships, in persecutions, in difficulties. For when I am weak, then I am strong'' (2 Cor. 12:9–10).

The power partner's control and ridigity permeate (usually unknowingly) the entire existence: with the mate, with God, with the church, and with self. The real source of all power, however, comes from turning self off and plugging in to Christ. Anything hindering that process robs a person of real power. The power partner operates not from a position of strength but from a position of personal weakness, often without realizing the length and breadth of such psychological and spiritual deception.

In the sea, the blowfish can appear to be powerful when it is not. The power partner is like the blowfish. Whenever a predator or seemingly hostile force presents itself, the blowfish pumps itself up to appear more powerful and intimidating than it really is. This pumping up is merely a cover-up. Though such actions may have certain benefits for the blowfish, the behaviors possess very definite disadvantages for the power partner—with God, with self, and with relationships.

During the aftermath of Hurricane Hugo, I was particularly struck by how the most impressive-looking and powerful grand old trees were uprooted or snapped like twigs. Yet smaller, less-obdurate trees bent with the winds, proving to be resilient in weathering the devastating fury of the storm. Similarly, the power partner is doomed to fall due to the insufficiency of the rigidity. And the fall of the power partner automatically affects other important people and valued relationships.

Denying Denial

Another very large problem confronting the power partner is called denial. (I'm not referring to the river in Egypt.) Denial is the ability to not see, or to dismiss as being inapplicable, something that is definitely present and operational. The coping mechanism of denial is the glue that holds everything together and allows continuance of dysfunctional processes.

Eubie Powers was a client who exhibited obvious and gross characteristics of a well-intentioned Christian who was rigid. When we reviewed the features of rigidity, he readily recognized them intellectually but saw only a few of them in his life. He rated himself as being a mildly rigid person. Of course, mild rigidity (also referred to as power-oriented) doesn't appear to be all that bad and is probably fairly widespread across the Christian community. But even at the mild level of rigidity, some very real concerns can negatively affect the person and the loved ones. Even a person who is mildly rigid is capable of blatantly rigid behaviors. The difference between a mildly rigid partner (power partner) and a mid-range or severe power partner is the difference in extent and intensity.

Eubie was beyond mild rigidity but just couldn't see it. He was confident that his mild rigidity was harmless and probably even necessary most of the time. His inability to see himself accurately and to understand, acknowledge, own, and amend his extent of rigidity cost him quality of relationships and eventually his marriage. Later, it also cost him his professional standing in the community and ruined his Christian witness.

Let me take a moment to plead that the information in this book is important to all Christians and vital to Christian relationships. Your mate may not be able to tell you of the need to learn, understand, and conquer all forms of rigidity or passive-dependency—in your life, in your marriage, in your home, in your church, and in your work. This respectful request is not a threat or demand but a love letter to you from someone who loves you very much and wants to see you fully blessed by Christ.

It is also a personal request from me. It really hurts me to see people who are committed to Christ and committed to their families shooting their wounded (with the very weapon intended to protect them). And there are many wounded around us—some bleeding internally who don't even recognize the extent of their injuries. We can be wounded, too, and like soldiers in the heat of battle, we may not notice the pain and damage. Please seek Christ's healing and protection. He loves you very much and went to the cross to take the beatings and punishment for you. The effects of sin in the world and the legitimate pain and suffering of life that we must confront are enough—we don't need to be participating in or creating unnecessary pain and destruction.

It is also a call to holiness. Rigidity and passive-dependency are treacherous stumbling blocks and barriers to growth in Christ. Any form of rigidity is a potential killer. Many times, however, it's not only the power partner who gets hurt; someone close may bear the brunt of the unrecognized personal and relational effects.

People don't like to think of themselves in a negative way, and rigid individuals resist receiving feedback that could be negative. Rigid persons will deny and/or minimize rigid traits about themselves and minimize passive-dependent traits in their mates.

Examine your life-style honestly.

Turn to the ''Pretest for Power Life-style.'' This pretest is only a rather rough guideline to obtain information about possible power-rigid processes in a person's life. Power people almost always score themselves less than do their mates taking the same test as if they were the power people. In fact, the contrast can be alarming if mates are allowed to be truthful without fear of retribution. A passive partner's scoring for a power partner is often more realistic than a power partner's

self-estimation. But no battles, please. The real answer probably is somewhere in between both scores.

The pretests for both power and passive life-styles are
straightforward, taking the testee at face value as being open
and honest (and trying to minimize denial). The pretest can be
manipulated or fooled, but it's not the test that is actually being
deceived. The pretest is designed only to get the testee into a
self-examining mind-set as the person honestly and prayerfully
studies the behaviors, characteristics, and effects of each life-
style presented and clarified throughout this book. A good
psychologist uses tests only to help make a diagnosis or clinical
decision. Similarly, individuals taking either pretest should give
more credence to the individual and circumstances surrounding
and supplementing the material suggested by the test.

Pretest for Power Life-style

Please answer the following items either true or false as applied
to you:

_____ 1. I am the one who decides what is viewed on TV.
_____ 2. I am the one in charge of allocating how to spend
household moneys.
_____ 3. My mate thinks that I have to have things my way.
_____ 4. My mate seems to think that I blame others for
things for which I am responsible.
_____ 5. It is easy for me to admit when I am wrong.
_____ 6. Others would describe me as being very open-
minded.
_____ 7. Sometimes my mate seems to feel intimidated by me.
_____ 8. I like to have the final say on a matter.
_____ 9. After everything settles from a conflict, I am usually
found to be right.
_____ 10. Things are either right or wrong.
_____ 11. There is one correct way for doing just about everything.
_____ 12. Compromise is only for politicians.

___ 13. It is easy for me to understand my mate's deeper feelings.

___ 14. I am regarded as being a teachable and approachable person.

___ 15. Sometimes I become jealous of my mate.

___ 16. When I make up my mind about something, that particular issue is closed.

___ 17. I have been described as being a patient individual.

___ 18. Things always go my way.

___ 19. I really don't like to be surprised.

___ 20. After an argument, I am usually the first one to say, "I'm sorry."

___ 21. I have been accused of being critical.

___ 22. I am always open to suggestions for change.

___ 23. There is one right way and many wrong ways for doing things.

___ 24. My mate would say that I have to be right about everything.

___ 25. I have never been accused of being stubborn.

___ 26. I am completely open and honest about myself with my mate.

___ 27. I see to it that I have a system of accountability in my life.

___ 28. I have been described as being forceful with my views.

___ 29. I make better decisions than my mate does.

___ 30. I have a need to be in control of most, if not all, matters that involve me.

___ 31. Tests like this are a waste of time.

Scoring for Power Pretest

Scoring: 1 point for each

True = 1, 2, 3, 4, 7, 8, 9, 10, 11, 12, 15, 16, 18, 19, 21, 23, 24, 28, 29, 30, 31

False = 5, 6, 13, 14, 17, 20, 22, 25, 26, 27

Score: _____

Free to be a servant-leader = 4 or less.

Relational power-passivity = 5 *and* mate's score of 6 or more on "Pretest for Passive Life-style." This power-passive dynamic minimally occurs in the relationship, but the relationship has allowed this person to assume the power role.

Power partner = 6-10. Mild forms of rigidity likely exist that could be problematic personally but can cause additional relational difficulties that aren't noticed (but felt injuriously by others).

Rigid person = 11-20. Mid-range rigidity suggests others are being negatively affected in a way that causes distancing and avoidance (by them, though the rigid person probably won't notice). Closeness and relational intimacy are probably being sacrificed.

Severe rigidity = 21-28. Severe rigidity suggests that there are many problems personally and relationally. Unfortunately, the severely rigid person will likely deny it all and will view tests like this one as "utter nonsense and a complete waste of time."

Emotional tyrant-dictator = 29 or more. This power level suggests little likelihood of change because the person is usually too fixed in the control role in its extreme. Power and control cannot be relinquished, and this person dictates everything in some form or another.

Understanding Rigidity

The major problem for the power partner is rigidity. The power partner may evolve into an inflexible bully using Christianity as a weapon. A continuum for the power-rigid dynamic illustrates the range of rigidity. See figure 2.1 for this range of behaviors.

Free to be	Relational	Power partner	Rigid person	Severe	Emotional
a servant-leader	power-passivity	(mild rigidity)	(mid-range)	rigidity	tyrant-dictator

FIG. 2.1. Continuum for the power-rigid dynamic.

As figure 2.1 depicts, power partners can be rigid in certain relationships alone, such as marriage (this would be referred to as relational power-passivity), they can possess rigid characteristics that range from mild to severe, and they can possess a unique combination of both. Any degree of rigidity affects their freedom and ability to be biblical servant-leaders and true followers of Christ.

A range of characteristics and behaviors is helpful in further clarifying and defining the power partner. This chapter focuses on defining this personality and understanding these descriptions. The more present and pervasive the characteristics and behaviors, the more severe the rigidity.

The power partner is not a deliberately bad person. The zeal to do the right thing and to stringently adhere to the correct course tends to overshadow other parts of life and leads to emotional and spiritual injury. One loving wife of a power husband stated it clearly, "He tries so hard to do what's right that he often misses out on other things—like feelings, respect for other people, and consideration of me."

To better understand rigidity conceptually and definitionally, it is helpful to think of clinical depression. Saying that someone is depressed can mean that the person is mildly depressed, feels down, or has "the blues." Or it can mean that the person is overwhelmed by sadness, hopelessness, and psychosis.

In thinking about the power partner, there is also a continuum. On one end of the continuum there is mild rigidity and on the other end there is severe rigidity.

I have developed a list of ten key characteristics of the power partner: mild rigidity would involve three, mid-range rigidity would involve five, and severe rigidity would involve seven or more. There is a range of meaning and intensity for each characteristic. However, it takes only the minimal criterion to qualify for any characteristic.

These characteristics of the power partner are presented in no particular order. All are important. Although there may be some overlap, there is also a unique component to each of the ten characteristics. The power partner has each thread interwoven into the fabric of the personality. Sometimes these characteristics confine themselves to one primary relationship. Each characteristic may not manifest itself in every situation, but it remains a recognized way of life.

The following list contains characteristics that are diagnostic and representative of the power partner (rigid personality). It should be noted that any one descriptor is adequate to positively designate the entire trait.

The power partner is

1. controlling and dominating.
2. blaming, unable to accept responsibility.
3. intimidating; the person tries to make significant others feel inferior or inadequate.
4. stubborn, unable to be reasoned with, close-minded, obstinate, and inflexible.
5. authoritative; the person is the final expert on a matter and is always right (in the person's opinion).
6. extremes-oriented; the person sees the world as black and white and is uncompromising.
7. rigid and legalistic and goes by the rules.
8. self-focused; empathy is impaired.
9. jealous, easily threatened, and defensive.
10. demanding and impatient.

1. The Power Partner Is Controlling

Modern technology has given us a quick and simple way of identifying who is the controller of the house. It's the person who always has the remote control for the television! It doesn't matter if anyone else is enjoying what's already on, the controller flips through the channels at the most inconvenient moments. The controller decides what is viewed and usually takes the choice seat in the room. In rare instances, the controller may allow others to watch something they want to see, but the complaints and negative comments generally spoil it for the others. Admittedly, this may not be a true litmus test for pinpointing the controller, but it's a good place to start!

The next place to check might be the checkbook. Who decides how to spend family income and tells what can and cannot be purchased? Again, this is not a surefire method for nailing the controller, but it's another good place to look.

People who like to have their way now and then don't really qualify as controllers. Controllers insist on having their way most, if not all, of the time. They not only control what goes on but also try to control everyone involved or at least see that nobody else takes control.

It is not always easy to detect controllers. They control directly, indirectly, or mixedly (directly *and* indirectly). The person who stands out the most or who appears to be the more dominating may not actually be the controller. It is easier to spot the direct controller who manages the mate with a clear, straightforward manner of rule. The indirect controller is outwardly calm, seemingly cooperative, but silently runs the show despite any focus upon the dissatisfied passive partner who ends up giving in to the power partner's quiet reign. The controller can also fluctuate between direct and indirect forms of governing.

Good leaders have in mind everyone's best interests.

Good leaders are not controllers. Leading is not necessarily controlling, though it can involve controlling behaviors. Controllers can do some leading, but good leaders do not require absolute control. Good leaders direct activities and events with the best interests of all concerned. Controllers are less concerned with others' best interests and more concerned with taking care of themselves. Motivation, and the concern for others ahead of themselves, distinguishes leaders from controllers.

The controller has to be in charge of things. Someone else can do the leading or do the work as long as the controller determines what happens all along the way. There is almost always some consequence—from pouting and sulking to yelling and harming—if the power partner is stopped from having control. The other party learns that it is easier for everyone concerned if the controller is allowed to run things. Unfortunately, there always is a penalty to pay at sometime or another. The penalty consists of some degree of loss of freedom or dignity—to one's task, to one's life-style, to one's self-concept, and/or to one's faith. These penalties, seldom consciously realized or understood, are interpreted as sacrifices. Such a sacrifice had been suffered by Wendy Trollins who endured it for many years, assuming it to be her Christian duty.

Mr. and Mrs. Trollins began marital counseling because of Wendy's weariness and resentment toward her husband, Ken. Over the years of their marriage, her resentment had soured into bursts of outrage and emotional and sexual withdrawal. She couldn't understand why she felt so terribly toward Ken. Though she could identify the source of her anger as being from Ken, she could not focus or express her animosity appropriately. The repressed feelings ended up coming out in other forms. Her anger toward Ken came out toward her children. Her anger also turned itself inward, becoming depression. When she caught herself lashing out at her innocent children, she became more upset and secretly resorted to the use of alcohol to try to get away from the ugliness of her situation. Alcohol only intensified her depression. Her destructive cycle worsened.

It didn't take long to discover that Ken was a very controlling husband. He controlled everything. Wendy was given an allowance, but she had no control over any of the family finances. She didn't even know Ken's income. When she needed groceries, Ken gave her a blank check made out to the grocery and told her the limit. If Wendy went five or ten dollars over that limit, Ken would pitch a fit and go into a long, demeaning tirade. Wendy eventually had to get part-time work to have some spending money of her own. She resented the time her job took away from being a full-time, at-home mother. (She and Ken had made an agreement that she would not have to work outside the home.) Wendy felt cheated and unimportant, yet she believed she should not feel that way. As Ken reminded her, she had so much for which to be grateful. The Lord certainly had blessed them. But something seemed wrong.

As we share in the Trollinses' life-style, we can get some idea of why their marital relationship wasn't working. Ken was a blatant controller who was easily exposed upon close examination. This unmasking, incidentally, is the very reason that controllers are reluctant to come for counseling. They don't appreciate a therapist's learning of the family dilemma or intervening in the existing way of living.

Just as there are different levels of being power partners, there are varying levels of being controlling partners. On the milder end of the controlling continuum are individuals who, without such obvious symptoms, still get their way most of the time. They are more subtle, and their mates are, therefore, more tolerant of the behavior. But it's the same poison—it just takes longer to do the job.

Controlling partners often hide behind labels that permit their actions. Such labels may be "protective husband"; "disciplinarian"; "priest"; "biblical leader"; "boss"; "smarter"; "responsible"; "authority"; "experienced"; "breadwinner"; "caretaker"; and so on. All of these labels may very well be legitimate. For controllers, however, the labels are a smoke screen for getting their way. Controllers may actually believe the label(s) created for each situation. But their motivation is wrong. They are trying to run things according to their own needs, even if these needs are unrecognized or unacknowledged. They may feel that they are being helpful, and to some extent, they may be.

One of the controller's rallying cries goes something like this: "I don't know why you don't appreciate all I have done for you." Another is this simple message: "You owe me." Controllers know how to manipulate, and they are not above tactics like making others feel badly in order to have their way. They are not necessarily aware of their manipulativeness. If confronted about manipulation, they'd protest and deny it loudly. Severe controllers become very antagonistic. They become verbally, emotionally, and/or physically abusive. Mid-range controllers do some of these things but, more often, threaten these things without following through. Mild controllers don't go nearly that far but may use emotional devices (e.g., lack of appreciation, disappointment, hurt, and guilt) as stratagems if it looks as if they may not get their way.

All of these characteristics must be consistent and continue in this pattern over time to truly fit the criteria of controller. There are times when the most humble and sacrificing servant must assume control over appropriate situations. That does not qualify such a person as a controller. The controller seems to perpetually dominate persons or situations.

Adlerian psychology has provided a helpful understanding of the controlling personality. This psychological approach can be useful even if it is not completely biblical (although a great deal of Adlerian psychology aligns nicely with a scriptural approach). Alfred Adler, a contemporary of Sigmund Freud, recognized the biblical truths of Romans 12:2 ("And do not be conformed to this world, but be transformed by the renewing of your mind, that you may prove what the will of God is, that which is good and acceptable and perfect" [NASB]) and Proverbs 23:7 ("For as he thinks within himself, so he is" [NASB]) and incorporated these truths into his psychological theory. Though he did not necessarily realize that the truths were biblical, he nonetheless built upon them. In a very real sense he should be considered the father of modern cognitive psychology. This school of psychology emphasizes that we filter all of our experiences and subsequent behaviors and feelings through cognitive glasses.

Live by God's truth as well as feelings.

Such an approach is beneficial to Christians in that it teaches we align our feelings and behaviors to be in accord with our thoughts and perceptions. Such a view reminds us not to go by feelings alone but to go by God's truth as found in Scripture. The ABCs of cognitive psychology teach, as articulated by Albert Ellis (an atheist), that the activating event (*A*) does not lead to the consequence (*C*) of that event. Rather, the belief (*B*) determines and influences the consequence of that event. Later cognitive psychologists concluded that our beliefs can be colored by our stored experiences and feelings. Among other things, that means we may experience reality and truth in a distorted way according to our unique cognitive spectacles. That also means some well-meaning Christians may color their view of truth by perceptions that may be based on something else, such as a life-style, personality, or psychological need. Psychological problems, however, do not excuse scriptural or moral duty, responsibility, or behavior.

Adler believed all behavior is purposeful. Even though it may not be consciously understood by individuals, their behavior is goal-directed. Behavior is consistent with life-style. One life-style, identified by Adler, is the controlling life-style. This life-style parallels the controlling characteristic of the power partner. Adlerian psychology clarifies that order is very important with this life-style. Unfortunately, the only acceptable order for controllers is their order. When there is this type of order, there is a false feeling of safety and security. The goal for controllers is to avoid humiliation. They do not like surprises. Therefore, they organize the world to keep surprises and chaos to a minimum by trying to control all that is around them.

So the first consideration in diagnosing a power partner is determining a controller characteristic. In terms of diagnosis, whether an individual is a mild, mid-range, or severe controller doesn't really matter. A person who is any of these fits the general requirement of controller and qualifies under this characteristic. A mild controller probably will be a mild power partner if the other minimal requirements are met as well. Likewise, a severe controller most probably is a blatant power partner if the other requirements are met as well. Usually, the more severe the controller, the more likely the person will meet more of the ten key characteristics of the power partner. One can be a power partner, however, without this particular characteristic.

(In my experience, it seems that men tend to outnumber women in overall characteristics of the power partner—at least in the context in which I deal with them: Christian marital and family counseling. However, in many cases the roles are reversed. Though I know of no research on this subject, perhaps this book will generate such.)

2. The Power Partner Is Blaming

The blamer is a faultfinder who acts superior and seems to say, "If it weren't for you, everything would be all right!" There is a quick test to gauge if an individual is a blamer. The blamer usually lacks two important words in the vocabulary: *I'm sorry*. It is very difficult for the blamer to utter these words and really mean them.

The blamer has to be correct all the time. One easy way to accomplish such a goal is to blame someone else for whatever happens. The blamer cannot accept responsibility or own the notion that he may have made a mistake.

It is not unusual to find blamers in counseling situations. They want to drop off their mates, have the psychological points and plugs changed and tires rotated, and then pick them up on the way home later that evening! If the problem is not fixed to their satisfaction, they blame the counselor for not doing the job right. Then they have a convenient excuse for not continuing counseling. A counselor who was any good in the first place would solve all the problems and life would be fine. This reasoning sounds a lot like the circular reasoning Groucho Marx used in considering membership in an exclusive club. He figured any club that would allow him to be a member wasn't worth joining in the first place!

Blamers have to be correct all the time. They shift the focus of responsibility onto someone else or something else. They find faults with others that are their own faults or responsibilities. Or they find faults in others to work as a smoke screen for detecting their own faults. If they can keep the spotlight on others, they avoid being more closely scrutinized. Sometimes this faultfinding is done by criticism. In interpersonal relationships, blamers can be quick to criticize the other person. By keeping the spotlight on the other person, blamers dodge their responsibility or role in a problem.

Blamers can range from being nagging, complaining, critical, or abusive to being quietly avoidant, constructively critical, disapproving, or mildly faultfinding. Even mild blamers choke on having to make an apology. Much of the time they won't apologize even if they have been clearly shown wrong. Many times they just drop the matter and silently go about their business, hoping all has ended and won't be brought up again.

Emma Poindexter had seen me for several sessions. She came alone, though her husband was invited. Manny Poindexter, Emma's husband, refused to attend counseling. By all of Emma's descriptions, Manny was a flagrant power partner. He was also very frustrated, angry, and depressed. What Emma told me that morning greatly concerned me but illustrates the way of the blamer.

Manny refused to get help for his worsening anger and depression. His self-treatment strategy seemed to consist of getting his anger out via blaming Emma for anything and everything that was unsatisfactory in their life together. He became more and more rigid, blaming, and verbally abusive to Emma.

That week Manny literally grabbed Emma by the shoulder, forced her up against a wall, and called her demeaning and critical names. He was trying to intimidate and frighten her while simultaneously making her feel guilty about her role of wife.

After his verbal explosion, Manny abruptly left the house. Emma was understandably upset, but afterward, she decided to go ahead with the plans she had made for the day. She and Manny had planned on going to a church luncheon later that afternoon. Emma went to the church luncheon alone, hoping that Manny might join her after he cooled down. He never showed. All of their friends at church asked for Manny, but Emma avoided the questions by vaguely stating that he had gone out and she hoped he would get back in time to join her at the luncheon.

Having somewhat cooled down, Manny returned home later that afternoon. He blamed Emma for being unavailable to him and for going out rather than staying home and working on their relationship. He really meant that he resented her going out to the luncheon and not becoming intimidated by his histrionics. The fact that she innocently went on without him infuriated Manny all the more. His way of handling his feeling was to blame Emma for her "insensitivity and unavailability." That Manny was abusive and disrespectful was not addressed. That Manny stormed out of the house and could not be found was seemingly immaterial. It was all Emma's fault. If she had been a better wife, the episode wouldn't have happened.

3. The Power Partner Is Intimidating

The power partner is intimidating. The person tries to make significant others feel inadequate, inferior, incorrect, mistaken, incompetent, or mentally or intellectually deficient.

Such intimidation goes beyond the characteristic of controlling in that the intimidator tries to emotionally blackmail significant others by fear. Intimidation can be used as a vehicle for controlling, but it can also be done for other reasons, such as issuing a nonverbal warning: "Don't mess with me!" The intimidator likes being in the one-up position. Many times this position is used to get or to maintain control. At other times it is used by the intimidator just to feel better about the self.

There is a certain recognition of dignity and respect when a judge enters the courtroom and those present are asked to rise. Similarly, the intimidator feels a certain exhilaration from the false perception of respect and fear from those intimidated. It artificially boosts a poor self-concept in a similar way that criticizing does for the blamer. The emotional argument goes something like this: "If I can't feel good about myself because I'm afraid others are better than I am, and I can't rise to their level, I'll bring them down to my level."

The message of the intimidator is "You don't measure up, but I do. I'm better than you." This message works in relationships at work, home, or school: "I have power and influence over you even when I'm not actively using it." Though intimidating is obviously related to controlling, it is also a unique quality in its own right. It can be compared to the pecking order at school or work. The person at the top gets to make all the decisions, but there is also something prestigious and powerful about simply being on top. At the least, it is far better than the indignation of being at the bottom.

Intimidators try to make others feel insignificant, inadequate, and inferior. One-upmanship is the name of the game. It can be done intellectually, vocationally, financially, educationally, emotionally, professionally, and/or physically. With the Poindexters, Manny emotionally intimidated Emma by making her feel inferior and inadequate in her role of the submissive wife. When his emotional tactics didn't work, Manny became physically intimidating and threatening. As hard as Emma tried to be a compliant mate, she often accepted without question Manny's accusations. She learned to feel a sense of false guilt not so much from her actions as from Manny's reactions.

There are two general types of guilt: true guilt (the individual has done something wrong and should appropriately feel guilty) and false guilt (the individual has done nothing wrong but feels inappropriately guilty). The Greek word for "guilt" is *hupodikos,* which means "to be brought to trial; to be liable to a charge or action for doing something wrong." A person is guilty, by biblical definition, when God's moral law is broken. False guilt is based on a false standard of righteousness. The blaming partner often triggers the other partner's false sense of guilt and then uses the guilt as a vehicle of intimidation.

Distinguish between false and true guilt.

You can't seem to really please an intimidator. If you do, you have passed the intimidator on the totem pole. Whatever you do is never quite good enough.

4. The Power Partner Is Stubborn

There are two sides to every coin. Determination is seen as a positive and healthy attribute, but the flip side is stubbornness. The power partner is stubborn but, at times, may seem determined. This partner usually cannot be reasoned with and is inflexible more often than not.

Stubbornness can be a deceptive characteristic, particularly for the Christian. In many legitimate areas of Christianity, the believer should be unyielding and determined. Such areas include the inerrancy and infallibility of Scripture, the virgin birth and deity of Christ, and Christ's perfect life on earth—the Lamb without spot or blemish. In such legitimate areas, an individual's obstinacy becomes a legitimate virtue. But the power partner's stubbornness goes beyond this. Unfortunately, it can often be interpreted as the virtuous side of the coin when it more accurately should be seen as a vice. The power partner is stubborn much of the time, not just at appropriate times.

As with the other characteristics, there is a range of stubbornness associated with the power partner. The mildly stubborn individual appears resolute and insistent, the mid-range individual appears inflexible and uncompromising, and the severe individual appears insistently dogmatic, arrogant, close-minded, and demanding. The severe individual greatly resents that anyone would even consider a different position and may verbally, emotionally, and/or physically attack the person who seems to challenge the position.

5. The Power Partner Is Authoritative

Power partners are authorities even in areas where they may not know what they are talking about. And the ones who do know something about the matter at hand fool others into yielding to them for the wrong reason. Just because people know something about one or two areas doesn't mean they are automatically authorities in other areas. Yet power partners fool themselves and others by such thinking.

Power partners are easily swayed by teaching that may sound authoritative, be it true or false. Since control is such a supreme issue for power partners, they perceive as dangerous anything that poses a threat to their feeling of control. If power partners can successfully label something (such as psychology) or someone (such as a spouse, employee, or prominent figure) as dangerous or as a threat to following Christ, they have seemingly defused the potential threat to their control. In so doing, they feel they have won the battle. Yet it may cost them the war.

Other power partners very much believe that their particular views are biblically sound to the exclusion of all others. They see it as their duty to warn the rest of the Christian community about the pitfalls of Christian living. They can become blinded to their own ways and leave a destructive path behind them without the slightest notion of the very damage they have done. And they do it all in the name of Christ.

Power partners lack the ability to develop healthy balance and godliness. They easily can become alarmists, and if something isn't black or white, the alarm goes off. But it doesn't go off just for appropriate circumstances; it goes off for every circumstance.

Power partners love structure and rules. Sometimes it feels so good to have rules that guidelines are made up just to feel good. Of course, this is not a conscious act. No one would ever admit to such a thing. But it happens. There is a feeling of safety in structure. Sometimes power partners' need for rules overpowers their thinking as to the correctness and appropriateness of the rules. This deceptive process can lead to letting someone else think for them. And where does God come into this? He may be left behind in the blind yielding to the god of "rule." This yielding to rules for the sake of following rules is exactly why Christ cautioned and admonished the Pharisees. The Ten Commandments are valid, given to us to follow for our best interests and protection, but the commandments themselves are not the object of our obedience or worship. Neither is Scripture per se. Jesus Christ is. Power persons blindly focus more on following the rules than on following the Giver of the rules or on reflecting Him. They enjoy the feeling of authority that rules provide for them. Deception and pride fuel their drive for authority.

Power partners are susceptible to false teaching, especially if the teacher seems authoritative. Again, the habit of needing a rule and going by rules can blind people to the actual truth of a rule. This is especially confusing if there is good and bad in a choice before them. For power partners, it's all-or-nothing thinking. An extremes-orientation is the focus of the next characteristic, but it works hand in glove with authority. It can be the vehicle that documents the right to possess and assert authority.

In 1980, I had the privilege of following Dr. Hans Selye at presentations of the CAPS (Christian Association for Psychological Studies) annual national convention in Toronto. Like so many others, I had admired his pioneering work in the area of stress. In fact, he is world renowned in the field and regarded by many as the father of the field of stress.

In this area, he has influenced my thinking. That doesn't mean I believe everything he has said nor do I endorse all his views. For the power person, this qualification is enough to totally discount and discard all of what Dr. Selye has bequeathed to science. That would be missing a lot and would be costly on a worldwide basis since his work has been so globally significant.

I'll never forget Dr. Selye's presentation. I'm not sure at what point he left the area of stress proper, but when he addressed points in the areas of ethics, morals, and religion, he missed the mark completely. I've seen it before. An authority in one field somehow wanders out of his area of expertise and feels he is also qualified in other areas when he is not. Though I rejected what he had to say in the related fields of ethics, morals, and religion, I retained much of his useful information on stress.

It is often amusing when television celebrities act as authorities on real-life issues based primarily on who they are as celebrities. Being a celebrity alone certainly doesn't qualify anyone to have expertise in another area, yet many viewers will believe what is said. You may recall one commercial that started off with a celebrity saying, "I'm not a doctor, but I play one on TV." He went on to try to convince viewers why they should choose the health-related product he represented!

We Christians have our own celebrities who do something like this. Good Bible teachers, distinguished pastors, skilled counselors, or favorite writers are not necessarily qualified to make statements outside their area of expertise. Our Lord must have referred to us as sheep because of how easily we tend to be led away by anyone in authoritarian clothing. We must be careful who we listen to and remember that we are responsible to examine what is said.

Good Bible teachers, advisors, or counselors take their audiences into the presence of Christ. Power persons merely take their audiences. They bask in the glory of their authority rather than enter into a heavenly audience by Christ's authority. They are not aware of it, and they would strongly deny it at the conscious level.

Good teachers take us into Christ's presence.

Authoritarians usually must have the final say on a matter. They are *always* right. They enjoy the power of being in a position of authority. They may surround themselves with others to create the impression of diversity, but the individuals tend to be more yes-men and yes-women than abundant counselors. Power partners who are severely authoritarian are more concerned with solidifying or preserving authority than upholding truth. That doesn't mean authoritarians can't or won't accomplish many good things for Christ. In fact, it behooves their role and image as authority figures to perform well for Christ. Sadly, though, the unconscious motivation is focused not only upon Christ but also upon power partners' needs and position of authority.

Such authoritarians can be found at home, school, or work. Arthur and Betty Terry had come to me for family counseling. It didn't take long to discover that Arthur was a severe authoritarian. His adolescent children told of an instance that illustrated and typified Arthur's rigid authoritarianism. During a family discussion, Arthur argued that Tanzania was in Australia. His teenage daughter, Diane, stated that she had just studied about Tanzania and that it was in Africa. Arthur became hostile and insisted that it was in Australia. His tone of voice and demeanor were meant to signal Diane to drop the matter and defer to his authoritative opinion. Diane, however, did not concede; she left the room quietly. She returned moments later with an opened encyclopedia showing Tanzania in Africa. Arthur became enraged, ripped the page out of the encyclopedia, and declared that the encyclopedia was wrong. Tanzania was in Australia!

There is a continuum for authoritarianism. Mild authoritarians appear knowledgeable and resourceful in many areas, but they are usually bluffing in certain areas without admitting limitations to themselves and/or others; mid-range authoritarians appear more expert and opinionated (usually offering opinions whether or not they are asked) across a broad and varied range within a particular field and/or across various fields; severe authoritarians appear to have to always be right (in their opinion) and resent divergent perspectives. The keys to differentiating rigid authoritarians from godly knowledgeable people are inward motivation and outward expression. Rigid authoritarians need to be right for themselves and their unconscious needs. They seek expression of authority as a sign of their position and as an inner signal to their self-concept. Godly knowledgeable people want to be right to honor God and His truth. It is not so important that their knowledge be recognized by others as long as God's purpose is honored.

6. The Power Partner Is Extremes-Oriented

The power partner is extremes-oriented, seeing things from one extreme or the other, and being unable to see any ground in between. Things are either all right or all wrong. There is no give-and-take, no moderation. In a technicolor world, the extremes-oriented partner sees only black and white.

To the extremes-oriented partner, the word *compromise* sounds heretical and antibiblical. It is, therefore, avoided in word and deed. Unfortunately, the price that is paid is frustrated or defeated relationships when conflict or negotiation is involved. And no worthwhile relationship can avoid some kind of conflict or disagreement! Intimacy becomes a matter of winning or losing. The power partner does not like to lose. So the power partner ends up winning the conflict but losing out in the relationship, winning a battle but losing the war.

If they feel that a source of teaching contains anything that may be Christianly suspect, extremes-oriented partners will automatically reject everything from that source. They have no ability to glean truths and weed out unhelpful or erroneous content. In some philosophical circles, this thinking is a good, rational approach. If there is one part false and many parts true, the whole is still false. It's sort of like reasoning that since somebody spit a little bit into my soup, none of it is any longer palatable. In most instances, this approach has merit, especially if it's my soup! But in other instances, the whole platter doesn't have to be thrown away because the cook accidentally served me one portion of liver or asparagus.

A devoted Christian told me that he could no longer read or appreciate the works of Arthur Pink because, in one work, Pink seemingly tolerated the gap theory of creation. Certainly, this is throwing the baby out with the bathwater! Pink provides so many other golden truths and rich materials that it would seem sinful to miss out on them because of a disagreement with one thing he said. But that is how the extremes-oriented power partner operates.

I have mentioned the name of psychologist Alfred Adler. Though I cannot agree with everything he says about psychology, I can appreciate many of his helpful and valuable teachings that align with Scripture. An extremes-oriented power partner would totally reject all Adler had to say. This total rejection would be due not to accurately contesting Adler's discovery of certain of God's truths but to the rigid personality's distortion of life.

Again, it is a matter of balance. It can be argued that using drugs can be both helpful and harmful. Where there are elements of both good and bad, power partners immobilize. They get stuck and look for others to lead them, or they flatly avoid or reject everything. Street drugs are obviously harmful and on one end of the scale; a doctor's prescription is helpful and on the other end of the scale. Though I'm speaking quite generally, and though there are other factors to be considered (such as seriousness of condition), power partners may reason that they should reject all drugs. In so doing, they tend to throw the baby out with the bathwater. They'll resort to this type of reasoning most of the time unless, perhaps, another trusted, rigid authority instructs them differently.

Of course, this is an unusual and blatant example, but you get the idea that power partners lose out because the world of choices is so self-limited. Obviously, you can feel fine about taking medication and still be a power partner. However, the more an individual struggles with this matter of control, the more aversive the notion of using medication becomes. The need for control is a core ingredient of the power partner.

In decision making, power partners become confounded when the decision process contains both good and bad, or helpful and harmful, components. New information involved in the decision process is rejected in favor of previously held positions. However, power partners can be influenced about the decision by others who seem to be rigid as well. They may accept new information or change from such authority. In fact, they may seek out other authorities, believed to hold similar views, to legitimize their stand. If there is some truth in what the rigid leader says, whatever else is said becomes truth also. Unfortunately, in the extreme sense, this tendency naturally leads to Jonestown or Waco experiences.

7. The Power Partner Is Rigid and Legalistic

Power partners are legalistic, going by the letter of the law and missing the spirit of the law. Legalistic partners are constrained to go by the rules, to play by the book, and to strictly adhere to the law. They can't bend rules or tolerate others who don't seem to toe the line. To legalistic partners, obeying rules is functionally more important than knowing Christ and His will for us.

Ben and Barbara Denny spoke to me about their relationship

with their adolescent daughter. Barbara felt frustrated with Ben, feeling that he was too strict. Their daughter, Bonnie, was sixteen years old and was a very compliant child, yet Ben never seemed satisfied with her. Ben assured us that he was very satisfied with his daughter and he loved her very much. Yet he knew that something was missing, and that puzzled him.

Barbara shared an incident from the previous week. Bonnie had asked permission to be out one evening until midnight. Ben reluctantly assented. Bonnie came home, meeting her father's curfew, and kissed her father good night. On her way upstairs to her bedroom she politely reminded her father of her obedience and said it wasn't quite midnight. Ben chastised her to hurry upstairs, insisting that she wasn't yet in bed. He suggested she would take time to wash, undress, brush her teeth, and do all the things she usually did (being not exactly sure what they were) that seemed to take up her time before actually getting into bed with lights off and covers up. Rather than be lovingly appreciative and encouraging of his daughter's obedience and desire to please him, Ben focused on the deadline. He missed the spirit of the law (her obedience and submission) and concentrated on the letter of the law (his time constraint).

It was a typical occurrence in their home. Something between father and daughter was slowly dying. A shell of an existence is the inevitable consequence of extreme legalism. The legalistic partner appears to care more for something than for someone. Over the course of time, mutual respect deteriorates, and tasks are done perfunctorily to keep order but with the loss of dignity and personhood. People end up going through the motions of everyday living, but there is no real life. The legalistic partner's god becomes compliance to the law. There follows an insidious and gradual distancing from the Lawgiver. Legalism seems like real spirituality, but it is oppressive and depressing. It is like a sheet of music without any instruments to bring it to life or a beautifully decorated present with nothing inside. It is idolatry.

Mildly legalistic partners appear orderly and organized on the outside, but a closer look reveals people who need a guidebook or a manual to follow in order to feel comfortable and secure. Without such clear and habitual structure, mildly legalistic partners function poorly. Organized partners do not need to be organized and orderly all the time; they use such structure to accomplish a goal. Mildly legalistic partners use organization and structure as a means of feeling protected.

Mid-range legalizers are intolerant of new concepts or ideas, reminding others of the virtues of tradition. "We never did it that way before" and "this is the proper way" are rallying cries. Mid-range legalizers like to sing the same hymns every Sunday and detest new ways of worship. They feel it is their duty to call others to task if they break away from the traditional way of doing things. They go by the book, and they become self-appointed umpires to see that no violations are committed.

Severe legalizers are close-minded and stubborn. They just won't see things any other way and won't even consider alternatives or compromise. Even when they are wrong, they cannot be approached. Of course, to them, they are not wrong anyway. They go by their interpretation of the book, not just by the book.

8. The Power Partner Is Self-Focused

Power partners are self-focused and selfish. They have impaired empathy and cannot put themselves in another's shoes. They are aware of situations or people who may deprive them of some right or who may not understand them or who may offend them. Yet it is very difficult for self-focused partners to tell if they are depriving others of their rights or if they are not understanding others or if they may be offending others. They find it easier to concentrate on tasks—often to the exclusion of the people associated with the tasks. The job becomes more important than people and feelings. They may also evidence narcissistic personality features.

Due to deep insecurity, self-focused partners concentrate too much on themselves and miss out on what is happening with others. They are more concerned with themselves than with others. When others are speaking to them, they usually are not really listening because they are readying their next response.

Mildly self-focused partners have trouble ministering to others. They are more concerned with being ministered to. They are more interested in what's going on inside themselves than about what's going on inside others. In relationships, they seem shallow and aloof. They appear concerned about making the right impression. They appear to have a lack of genuine concern for others' feelings (though they can appear to be affected).

Mid-range self-focused partners see themselves as leaders with unique abilities. They are less interested in leading for the sake of helping others and more interested in self-aggrandizement. They lead so that others will follow them. They tend to take advantage of others and exploit relationships and situations. They are especially good at taking advantage of spouses or significant others. When trying to minister to others or to implement some plan or program, it has to be done in a certain way that fits their criteria, purpose, or understanding.

Severely self-focused partners exhibit many of the characteristics of a narcissistic personality disorder. There may be a grandiose sense of self-importance, a sense of entitlement, a disregard for the rights of others, and/or a marked lack of empathy. There may also be fantasies of unlimited success or achievement, the need for constant positive attention and admiration, and exaggerated statements of importance or accomplishment.

Many times self-focused partners leave behind them a trail of shattered lives and situations without a clue or a concern of their impact. Even if others could tell of their pain, power partners wouldn't really hear. Even if those people could show their wounds, power partners wouldn't really see.

9. The Power Partner Is Jealous

Because of deep feelings of insecurity and low self-esteem, power partners are jealous. They are easily threatened and possessive. Because of jealousy, they often make it difficult for their mates to enjoy outside relationships. They resent a spouse's involvement in situations that lend support to the spouse's ego strength. This includes, but is not limited to, friendships, family, and church involvement.

They may be very private and, at times, secretive. Openness and honesty elude jealous partners. They seem to be open and honest about most things but not about themselves. Actually, they are open only about things they want to talk about or want to impress upon others. They are defensive and guarded. They can become upset and angered and feel betrayed if mates reveal information about their lives without expressed consent.

By their secrecy, they are more likely to commit sins of omission rather than perpetrate sins of commission. They cannot share themselves. There is poor, or even no, accountability. In relationships, they give what they want to give and not much else. Intimacy in relationships is lost.

No one really knows what is going on inside jealous partners, and they orchestrate their lives to ensure this private existence continues. One person may know something about the jealous partner, and someone else may know something else. But no one person knows much about the jealous partner (outside the marital relationship). Most people would be surprised to learn of this person's jealousy because it doesn't fit the external picture. Others know only as much as the jealous partner will allow. The jealous partner is not usually aware of the extent of the emotional and relational seclusion and privacy.

Coinciding with possessiveness is suspiciousness. Jealous partners have difficulty trusting others. During times of marital stress, they may imagine that spouses are disloyal or unfaithful.

Bill and Irma Suggs had been seeing me for marital therapy. Due to Bill's history of being a severe power partner, Irma's ability to respond sexually to him had greatly diminished (as is one such natural consequence of relationships with power partners). As if that wasn't bad enough, Irma had been injured in an automobile accident and had chronic back pain.

Bill became increasingly suspicious of Irma's decreased interest in sex. Rather than accept that Irma's physical pain from the accident and her emotional pain from their deteriorating relationship had caused lack of sexual interest, Bill suspected there must be something or someone else involved. Irma discovered that Bill had their apartment bugged! Bill was convinced that there was another man. When his suspicion didn't pan out, Bill began to believe there might be a homosexual relationship with one of Irma's friends.

10. The Power Partner Is Demanding

Power partners are demanding, with no patience or very little patience. They are easily frustrated and expect others to remedy whatever may be the source of distress for them.

Demanding partners can be exacting and cautious. But they want things, and they want them right away, and they want them done correctly (according to their standards). They have little tolerance or use for those who can't meet their expectations.

Mildly demanding partners appear insistent, confident, and/or assured but not forceful. They have some degree of tolerance for other viewpoints (though they usually expect them to prove inferior to their own or to fail). Mid-range demanders are more zealous and persistent with viewpoints and demands, appearing arrogant and intolerant of different views. Severe demanders believe it's their way or no way, and they forcefully push and impose their demands on others.

Tallying Rigidity

Mild power partners exhibit three or more of these ten criteria. Mid-range (five) and severe (seven) power partners most likely won't consider such things, and they won't be willing to examine themselves. Mild power partners will be willing to do some examination, but mid-range and severe power partners will fight such examination unless no other options are available and their way is no longer working. But those close to them will recognize these characteristics right away. (Clinical judgment based on the pretest plus careful examination of the ten criteria plus knowledge of the individual involved should take precedence over the pretest information alone.)

There is likely some degree of rigidity in every Christian. There ought to be. Our view of the world, seen accurately through Scripture, the working of the Spirit, and the accountability of the body, is the right view! But this is a balanced Christian view. Power partners carry this view to extremes and cannot tell they are out of balance. They believe they are very right, and they will fight, religiously, for their cause. But this is not biblical Christianity. This is a cancer that destroys individuals, relationships, marriages, families, faith, and life.

Our God is an amazing God who can accomplish great miracles. There is hope for the power partner and most rigid Christian alike! Yet unless Christ actively steps in, the power partner is very tough to deal with. Christ does not push Himself on anyone, He waits for us to come to Him. Coming to Christ, or anyone else, is very difficult for the power partner. But at some point, this has already occurred, so there is hope.

There is hope for the rigid power partner!

Power partners like to look like they have their Christian walk together, and they are cruising along with abundant living. That isn't the case. But only those close to them could detect this, and they seem confused. Others are kept at a distance. They see only what power partners want them to see.

This book is written to help power partners and their families recognize that power partners are not really looking for any substantive help. Yet if power partners can be identified, and if they can be encouraged to help themselves and their families through a higher call to Christian life from God, real help is available.

In other ways, power partners and their families are like alcoholics and their families. Alcoholics are not highly motivated to change or seek help unless the situation becomes so intolerable they are forced to change or seek help. Alcoholics can withstand a great deal of intolerance. But others may make the alcoholism more tolerable; enabling spouses may blindly encourage the destructive cycle, believing they are merely being helpful, submissive, and loving spouses. Similarly, there are enablers for power partners. Through them, real help may become a reality. But it involves confrontation, loving toughness, determination, and obedience to Christ. Unfortunately, there are only two options for enabling spouses: one leads to loving toughness, and the other leads to a cancerlike process that is spreading and deathly. The next chapter addresses the role of spouses of power partners and the inherent dilemma of the relationship. Later chapters address the issue of how to help power partners change.

Chapter 3

THE PASSIVE PARTNER

The entire family frantically ran into the farmhouse and barred the door. Big Jake was coming! His reputation made the likes of Billy the Kid, Jack the Ripper, and the Incredible Hulk seem like schoolboys. He was seven feet tall and weighed 390 pounds.

With one sweeping blow he smashed in the wooden door, ripping the framework apart at the same time. Before the farm owner could load his double-barreled shotgun, Big Jake grabbed it and bent the barrel into a question mark. He picked up the farmer with one hand and carried him outside. Drawing a small circle, Jake snarled, "Stay in this here circle and y'won't get kilt!"

Jake immediately turned and ravaged the farmhouse. He wrote graffiti all over the house, then set the barn on fire. He yanked the farmer's wife into both arms, but when she screamed and passed out, Jake laughed and rode off.

Minutes later, the farmer's wife awakened and ran out to the farmer. "Are you all right? Why in the world didn't you do anything? Didn't you see what all he did? What's wrong with you?"

The farmer looked her squarely in the eye and retorted, "Oh, yeah? He's not so tough. When he wasn't looking, I stepped out of the circle three times!"

What a wimp!

Passive partners and wimps are more closely related than is readily apparent. A wimp is a passive partner carried to extreme. Figure 3.1 illustrates how a passive partner, a satisfier, a wimp, and an emotional slave are different versions and intensity/behavioral levels of the same thing. All passive partners are capable of engaging in wimp behaviors! It is not so easy to view the sacrificial acts of the passive partner as being wrong. Yet not all sacrifices are right. A major focus of this book is to disclose how such mistaken notions of sacrificing are deceptively destructive and dishonoring to God.

Free to be a servant-leader	Relational power-passivity	Passive partner	Satisfier	Wimp	Emotional slave

FIG. 3.1. **Continuum for passive-dependency.**

Unacceptable Sacrifices

Let's briefly consider the story of Cain and Abel (see Gen. 4:1–17). Cain's intentions seemed to be good and honorable when he brought his offering (sacrifice) to the Lord. Cain was a tiller of the ground (like his dad) and brought an offering of the fruit of the ground. But the Lord rejected Cain's sacrifice and accepted Abel's. It was a blood sacrifice that was needed. What Cain thought was a good and appropriate sacrifice was not. So we learn very early in Scripture that sacrificing behaviors are not necessarily good things and can be wrong.

There is certainly a proper use, practice, and understanding of sacrifice. It is one of the key concepts in Christianity. I am referring to the mistaken implementation of sacrifice—sacrificing wrongly under the guise of correctness. Hosea gives additional clarification that sacrifice can be done wrongly and that it is not necessarily the right thing to do for a given situation. God is interested in our hearts, not our sacrifices: "For I delight in loyalty rather than sacrifice, and in the knowledge of God rather than burnt offerings" (6:6, NASB). Jesus refers to this passage on several occasions (see Matt. 9:13; 12:7). God is interested in our knowing Him and following Him by faith and obedience.

God looks at the heart.

When the sacrificial acts of the passive partner are discussed in this book, they do not refer to a priest, or to a believer, carrying out an appropriate spiritual function or discipline; they refer to an individual who unnecessarily, inappropriately, and unbiblically sacrifices self. Passive partners are usually wonderful people who are liked, enjoyed, and appreciated by others. They can learn to perform sacrificing behaviors to gain that acceptance and approval by others. That is the very danger of being a sacrificer: doing good things for the wrong reason. At this point the good things are no longer sacrifices in the Abel sense; they become Cain sacrifices. Remember that Cain thought that his sacrifice, based on what he thought was right, would be good and acceptable, but it was not.

Christ looks at the sacrificer's heart. The key to sacrificial love and obedience to Christ is motivation and heart attitude. The question to ask yourself is a penetrating one that must honestly and accurately probe the depths of your intentions and actions: Is this giving of yourself based upon reflecting Christ and following Him completely, or is it determined or influenced by other factors, such as unrecognized psychological needs?

The concept of a sacrificing passive partner, as used in this book, alludes primarily to the kind of sacrificing that Cain did. Abel's sacrifice was pleasing and acceptable to the Lord. Abel's sacrifice removed Abel from the process and focused exclusively on giving God what God said He wanted. However, even what seems to be an Abel sacrifice can be sacrificing wrongly in relationships, especially if such actions reinforce codependency or a mate's dependency (as will be explained and clarified later). Cain's sacrifice put Cain in the process of doing what he thought was right when it wasn't based accurately on God's directives. Passive-dependency (which includes the passive partner, satisfier, and wimp) is self-focused rather than Christ-focused.

A Rough Test

The "Pretest for Passive Life-Style" is intended only to provide a rough guideline for the concepts discussed from the passive-dependent continuum, to give a basic idea of how the testee falls within the broad range of passive-dependency.

When passive partners go beyond appropriate marital sacrifice and submission, they mistakenly put others ahead of themselves due to their unrecognized needs to be personally accepted and approved. When passive partners go to the extreme ends of the passive continuum, allowing themselves to become relational doormats and incorrectly justifying passivity as being good, submissive, or biblical, they in effect become emotional doormats! More often, passive partners will engage in various forms of behaviors associated with being passive without necessarily moving to that extreme position of becoming an emotional slave. If these same behaviors continue consistently over time, however, they may very well need to consider such a designation. Of course, all these behaviors and descriptions are perversions of healthy, biblical models for living and are to be avoided.

The term *wimp* better expresses the negative component of the concept whereas the term *passive partner* sounds like it may be a good thing when, in the context of passive-dependency and codependency, it is not. One is obviously more blatant than the other, but both are wrong. Though wimp is an exaggerated personification of the passive partner concept, it emphasizes and more readily clarifies and connotes the destructive components of the passive-dependent life-style.

I hope *wimp* and *emotional slave* are understood to be terms that are deliberately used to emphasize the extreme and unacceptable life-style and behaviors of the passive-dependent individual. Even a mildly passive partner can commit grievous wimp behaviors. That is the intention of the use of these terms. If we find them bothersome or annoying, let's agree to direct our energies and resentments toward detecting and changing all forms of passivity—in our personalities, in our relationships, and in the church.

Pretest for Passive Life-Style

Please answer the following items either true or false as applied to you:

_____ 1. I tend to wait for things to happen rather than initiate things.

_____ 2. I always say exactly what I mean.

_____ 3. Others view me as a leader.

_____ 4. I try to avoid conflict whenever I can.

_____ 5. I am more concerned about how things affect others than how those things affect me.

_____ 6. I seek approval in relationships.

_____ 7. I am easily taken advantage of.

_____ 8. I can be very assertive when I need to be.

_____ 9. If something goes wrong, I tend to take the blame for it.

_____ 10. I tolerate a lot of disrespect before I say anything about it.

_____ 11. It's hard for me to say no to others.

_____ 12. What others think of me matters a great deal to me.

_____ 13. I have a lot of self-confidence.

_____ 14. It's easy for me to make decisions that involve others.

_____ 15. I try not to make any demands on others.

_____ 16. Others are more important than I am.

____ 17. I fear being abandoned or left alone.

____ 18. It's easy for me to express any disagreement with others.

____ 19. It's easy for me to make decisions without seeking help from others.

____ 20. I always try to please others, even if I disagree with them.

____ 21. I'm afraid to be completely truthful with my mate about my mate's degree of rigidity in our relationship.

Scoring for Passive Pretest

Scoring: 1 point for each

True = 1, 4, 5, 6, 7, 9, 10, 11, 12, 15, 16, 17, 20, 21

False = 2, 3, 8, 13, 14, 18, 19

Score: _____

Free to be a servant-leader = 5 or less.

Relational power-passivity = 6 *and* mate's score of 5 or more on "Pretest for Power Life-Style." The relationship has allowed this person to assume the passive role.

Passive partner = 7-10. This person is too preoccupied with pleasing others and rationalizes behavior to be good and biblical when these actions probably are not completely healthy or biblically motivated. The likelihood is that this person is a pleaser who is often taken advantage of (by wimping out).

Satisfier = 11-15. This person becomes a living sacrifice for very wrong and unbiblical reasons. This person mistakenly puts others ahead of self due to unrecognized needs and a great need to be personally accepted and approved. The likelihood is that this person can legitimately be considered a prewimp with regular wimping out episodes. The person tries to avoid all conflicts (keeping the peace) and to satisfy others as a means of doing so.

Wimp = 16-19. This person goes even further, becoming a doormat and justifying wimpery as being good, submissive, or biblical. The likelihood is that this person wimps out most of the time.

Emotional slave = 20 or more. This person is chained and bound emotionally to codependent passive-dependency. The likelihood is that this person almost always wimps out.

Understanding Extreme Passivity

Walter and Cindy Cox brought their adolescent daughter, Peggy, for counseling. She had recently been expelled from the Christian school she had been attending. She had problems with drugs and alcohol, and she had been caught stealing a car after a long joyride with friends. Peggy had a string of problem behaviors that seemed to be worsening.

Walter handled the problem by adding two more weekly Bible studies to his two existing Bible study groups. He particularly enjoyed rising very early every morning to be alone and prepare for his next group. Unfortunately, he zonked out early every night due to his 5:00 A.M. wakeup for solitude and study. He had little time for Cindy and Peggy, abandoning them to deal with Peggy's problems on their own. In actuality, he was avoiding his family. He could not control what was happening with his family, so he dove headlong into something he could control. Leading Bible study groups also made him feel like a good Christian. But he was hiding—sticking his head in the sand.

Though Walter was deeply affected by all that was occurring in his family, he succumbed to wimpery. He followed his natural instincts down the wrong trail.

Cindy tearfully complained of her feelings of frustration and abandonment. She was burning out. She had been carrying the family emotionally for quite some time. She was a very responsible person in most situations. But she wouldn't confront

Walter. As bitter and depressed as she felt, she could not be direct with him. She feared his response. Every time she had ever tried to approach him about similar feelings, he became angry and made her feel rejected. Besides, Cindy felt he really didn't need her and could conceivably leave! She reasoned that she had better not make any waves. So she kept her feelings inside, and she left Walter alone.

Dysbiblical Passivity

You guessed it! Passivity of the first degree. Cindy also tried to do what she thought best. Though her giving in kept the peace, it did nothing in the long run to address or rectify the problem. Passively giving in slowly reinforced the problem.

Why are we talking about passivity? Because power partners tend to marry passive partners. (They can work for them, too.) It is a dysfunctional relationship from the beginning, and the problems will surely surface at some point. And the scary but ironic part is, if the relationship is likely to successfully change, it usually falls on the shoulders of the passive partner.

Any Christian can be passive. There is surely some degree of passivity in all of us. Perhaps it was the time you tried to approach the boss about a raise but wimped out when he looked at you and chewed on his stogie the way he may bite off your head. Or perhaps it was the time when you were too polite to state your opinion on abortion to a neighbor or fellow employee when the subject came up. Or maybe, just maybe, you missed an opportunity to witness for Christ because others were around who may not have been very receptive or because you felt embarrassed or because you didn't know exactly what to say or because you felt you needed some more special training to share your faith or because you didn't feel like speaking up at the time.

It doesn't take much prodding to recall times when we all have wimped out. Wimping out is not necessarily sinful, though it can lead to sins of omission. But when it becomes a way of life, it goes against the grain of mature Christian living. And it can cause all kinds of relational, emotional, and personal problems. It also attracts power partners.

Patience and gentleness are not passivity.

Can you imagine Jesus being passive? Some folks do. Some Christians do and don't even realize that they do. These same folks distort Scripture to allow their own wimping out! We must not confuse such virtues as patience, gentleness, kindness, and self-control with passivity.

We can psychologically filter experiences and perceptions in ways that align with our deeper, and perhaps unrecognized, emotional needs. In our example, Walter did exactly that. His deeper need was to avoid conflict because of his deep feelings of inadequacy and insecurity, thereby maintaining an illusion of control over the situation. Yet Walter believed he was acting responsibly as a model Christian. In reality, he was passively giving in and not recognizing his behavior was based on his deeper needs.

Distortions of God

Freud suggested that we create God due to our own neuroticism to feel some kind of control over our world. For Freud, God was created by our own minds! What a perversion of the truth! That is not at all what I am saying. Rather, we Christians are capable of placing onto God personal characteristics and traits from our human experiences. Sometimes we may create our own perspective of God, theology, or scriptural interpretation based on our unrealized psychological needs and experiences.

One way we may do this is to view our heavenly Father as we

experienced our earthly, biological fathers. Of course, this is not done wholly (or holy) or consciously. We can tend to experience certain aspects of our dads. For example, one devoted believer shared that his father was the kind of dad who felt his primary responsibility was to provide for his family. Unfortunately, the dad spent most of his time away from home and on various jobs. Everyone knew where he was—out working. He would often come and watch part of his son's Little League game and then drive off—off to work. That dad showed his love, care, and concern for his family through perpetual work. The son grew up, accepting Christ as his Lord and Savior in his early twenties. In his fifties, the son continues to struggle with his concept of God, which he learned from his dad. For the son, God was too busy to be available to him. God was so busy running the universe that He seemed remote, distant, and unavailable. On the positive side, the son never questioned God's love and care for him. His father taught him that God was faithful.

Another believer shared part of her experience with her dad. He was a stern disciplinarian who ruled the home with very real consequences for his children's lack of obedience. He could be harsh and stern, but not at all abusive, with his disciplinary measures. He was showing his love for his family by teaching and enforcing discipline and responsibility. This woman still struggles with her concept of God based on her experience with her dad. She views God as hiding behind a cloud, monitoring her every move, waiting for her to make a mistake so He can zap her with lightning bolts! Again, this is not done consciously. On the positive side, the dad made it easier for his daughter to understand God's sovereignty. Her dad was a big, strong man who provided every physical need. She never worried or questioned his provisions for her.

We, as Christians, need to base our concept of God upon His Word as illuminated by His Holy Spirit. Power partners have a difficult time with this idea. They think they are doing it correctly, even to the point of being adamant and dogmatic about their position. Power partners' personalities are dogmatic and authoritarian. Yet rarely are their views exactly biblical. Rather, they tend to suit their unique need or circumstances. Power partners are self-focused and cannot see that they are self-focused. And power partners are not very tolerant of other views. Even if another Christian believes 99 percent the same, power partners will reject the Christian due to their extremes-oriented mind-set. For power partners, you are either all right or all wrong.

Distortions of Scripture

Similarly, passive partners unconsciously distort their view of God and Scripture. Passive partners often tend to see God as being passive and quiescent; they tend to see Scripture as commanding them to wimp out in some form. In many situations, both the power partner and the passive partner interpret Scripture the way that best justifies their continued life-styles around their unrecognized needs.

Though the next chapter specifically identifies characteristics of the passive partner, one obvious characteristic is passivity. Accordingly, the passive partner interprets Scripture in a passive way: Scripture says to turn the other cheek and not make waves. Admittedly, there are appropriate times for such behavior. For the passive partner, however, such passivity occurs most of the time and becomes a way of life. There is no balance such as characterizes the life-style of the biblical Christian.

Jesus certainly taught that we are to turn the other cheek (see Matt. 5:39; Luke 6:29). And He knew how to keep quiet at appropriate times (see Matt. 27:14; Acts 8:32). Yet He also knew how to speak up and confront people at appropriate times (see Matt. 3:7; John 2:13–16; 18:22–23). Among other things, Jesus could be tender, gentle, compassionate, loving, confrontational, patient, demanding, submissive, authoritative, and determined at the appropriate times. But Jesus was no wimp.

They Exist, Therefore I Am

Another popular teaching that particularly appeals to passive partners is the concept of denying self. Many passive partners define themselves in relation to others and have no concept of a self. They can't answer the question "Who am I?" They have a psychological need to put others ahead of God *and* themselves. Their unrecognized self-talk is, "I'm a Christian, therefore I don't exist." But the message of John 3:16 is that they *do* exist. However, the idea of denying self gives legitimacy to their wimpery, and it paints them as suffering saints. It is gratefully received and appreciated by the person who benefits most from it, that is, the other person in the relationship: the power partner. The concept of denying self, however, is a legitimate and central component of biblical Christianity. Again, it is a matter of balance. It is also a matter of motivation. The passive partner's motives are wrong in using this concept to justify continuing wimpery.

Some well-meaning Christians believe that denying self is sufficient. Martin Luther found that the extreme action certainly wasn't the answer. The practice of self-denial, however, seems to have some truth, especially when secular psychology and the media push the opposite concept of hedonistic narcissism or, at best, reciprocal pseudoaltruism (helping one another help ourselves). If it feels good, do it! Be all you can be! Look out for number one!

It's OK to care for yourself.

But denying self alone, even as a reaction against the zeitgeist of secular humanism and New Age teaching, is still insufficient and unbalanced. Living a life of self-denial by itself constitutes idolatry and is no more functionally valid than Eastern philosophies and worldviews that teach the emptying of oneself while denying the God of the Bible. Denying self does not mean hiding from truth or the effects of personal or relational woundedness.

Passive partners selectively read Luke 6:31 as "do to others." But there is more. It further says "as you would have them do to you." Passive partners read Matthew 22:39 as "love your neighbor." But there is more. It further says "as yourself." In these passages and throughout Scripture, balanced Christianity is taught. Further, it is assumed that we will care for ourselves. It's okay to do that! You are worth much to God! This is a difficult teaching for passive partners. Biblical Christianity mandates that we do both: care for ourselves and care for others simultaneously. Passive partners put self out of the picture completely. But it is not done with the appropriate motivation. It is done (unconsciously) for self-protection and for self-preservation of the passive life-style.

There is a rightful and appropriate motivation for self-denial. Self-denial is step one of a two-step process. Without step two, step one is incomplete. Biblical Christianity teaches that we deny self to put on Christ. The goal of self-denial is to become Christlike.

The power partner and the passive partner represent two extremes along the continuum of loving care. The power partner is on the end that focuses entirely on self, and the passive partner is on the end that focuses entirely on others. Neither is doing either for the right reason. Rather, both are emphasizing their particular focus as a means of self-protection.

Giving to Get

The passive partner gives to others and ignores self as a means of gaining their approval or avoiding disapproval and rejection. Such outward behavior allows the passive partner to feel safe and secure. It's a false feeling of safety and security, but it's all there is!

The power partner focuses on self and deemphasizes the

value or importance of others. The power partner also does this as a means of self-protection, though externally appearing to need no protection. The power partner can often present a very "together" facade, which usually fools all but those closest to the partner (who are also affected by their relationship). The power partner uses the passive partner to meet selfish relational needs while simultaneously devaluing the passive partner's importance. Down deep the power partner fears hurt and rejection. Feeling insecure, inadequate, and fearful, the power partner tries to minimize the need for others so that their power to hurt is minimized.

The biblical concept of self-denial as applied to the passive partner and the power partner would mean to quit being passive and rigid and learn of balanced Christian living with appropriate motivation. This in itself is still insufficient. They must then put on Christ. Motivation for change is to please God and to grow into the image of Christ (see Rom. 8:29; 2 Cor. 3:18; Eph. 4:14–15).

Neither the power partner nor the passive partner is really very interested in change—at least not initially. As their relationship continues over time, however, it begins to take its inevitable toll. The effects of this toll usually hit the passive partner first and hardest. The power partner may feel that things are pretty good and may be able to withstand a great deal of discomfort—especially since the passive partner is bearing most of the effect of the relational discomfort. The passive partner becomes an enabler for the continuing roles and functions of the relationship. As long as the passive partner can take it, the power partner can keep dishing it out! "Besides," argues the passive partner, "what right do I have to take care of myself? That's not Christianity, right? We've all got our crosses to bear. What would others think? What would the church think?" ("What would the power partner think? What might the power partner do?")

Again, the matter is motivation and balance. Our motivation should be to become like Christ. What did He do? What would He do?

Pure Giving

It goes without saying that Jesus loved others and gave Himself ultimately for others that we might be reconciled to God. That He also gave Himself to others relationally is clearly demonstrated in Scripture. Yet there was a balance. He ate and slept, too. On one occasion He slept while his friends panicked about the tossing of the waves all around their boat (see Matt. 8:24–25; Mark 4:35–38). A good passive partner would never have slept in the first place. It's against the first law of thermopassivity to actually take care of oneself, especially if there is anyone else around with any possible need or demand. Second, the passive partner would be doing whatever the others thought would be necessary to make them feel better about what was happening. That's the second law of thermopassivity: always make others feel the way they need to feel. (Needless to say, the passive partner does not apply these laws to other passive partners, who are automatically excluded under the no-count provision of the Hypocritic Doormat Oath.)

The passive partner would argue that Jesus could not have taken time for Himself at all. That would be selfish and unchristian. Yet we know from Scripture that Jesus did do things for Himself, and it was okay. For example, He would often go off alone to pray and commune with the Father. He did that "selfish" type of thing even if it was inconvenient or worrisome to those who were with Him (see Mark 1:35–37; Luke 4:42; 5:15–16; John 12:36). Obviously, it wasn't really selfish. It's okay for us, too, as long as it is appropriately balanced with giving, submitting, and serving. The idea is balanced Christianity.

Christ's Example

Scripture shows us that Jesus loved people and crowds, and He loved to receive people and crowds. Yet He knew how to set limits, too. Mark 14:32 documents that Jesus told His disciples to wait as He went off to pray. Though He took Peter, James, and John along with Him, He nevertheless set limits for the other disciples. Luke 9:28–36 records that Jesus did the same type of thing, going off alone with Peter, James, and John.

It's OK to set limits.

In Mark 3:7–10 and in Mark 4:1, we see Jesus setting limits again with those about Him. He physically set limits with the crowd. He got in a boat so that the crowd was limited in access to Him. Does that mean He was experiencing a change of heart? Not at all. He is showing us that we can take care of ourselves, set limits with others, and still love them and serve them at the same time. This is balanced biblical Christianity. It's not an either-or situation; it's a both-and situation. You can care for yourself and others at the very same time and still be quite biblical. (The power partner who is extremes-oriented will resist this point. The passive partner will find it hard to believe.)

Misusing Scripture

The passive partner interprets the beatitudes in a self-justifying, though incorrect, manner, viewing the meek as the passive partners. But the appropriate understanding of meek means being mild, patient, and long-suffering in righteousness and trust—not in avoidance and doubt. Similarly, the passive partner misuses the Philippians 4:13 passage ("I can do all things through Him who strengthens me" [NASB]) to play the martyr role with passivity. In this passage, Paul is not talking about being superhumans and enduring everything that life throws at us. Rather, the context suggests that he is referring to his ability to get along with modest means, hunger, and suffering. Further, the passage does not imply that Christians are to learn to be content with ungodly behaviors or situations. It is not an excuse to be passive.

Another common misuse of Scripture for the passive partner comes from Luke 6:27–31. The passive partner focuses exclusively on the first part of the passage, which emphasizes turning the other cheek. This passage seems to justify, to the passive partner, never standing up for yourself or for what's right. Again, it's a matter of context. We'll see in the passage below that Jesus didn't just look the other way to keep the peace. That is, however, what the passive partner does. The passive partner wants to avoid conflict. Biblical Christianity sometimes demands that we enter into conflict and not sell Christianity short to avoid it.

The last section of Luke 6:27–31 is the golden rule: "Do to others as you would have them do to you." This principle is directly related to the "turning the other cheek" principle. Yet for the passive partner, it seems to be juxtaposed: "Do for others even if it means letting them slap you, or righteous living, around." Obviously, this is not the point Scripture is making. Scripture doesn't contradict itself. "Doing for others as you would have them do for you" implies a certain standard of care for ourselves. We are not to completely give up ourselves to satisfy the worldly needs of others. We are not to provoke or aggravate others unnecessarily, nor are we to be too quick to take offense from others. We are to expect and to endure some degree of injustice, misunderstanding, persecution, anger, suffering, and rejection.

But there are limits. If others take offense at our biblical position or our biblical life-style, we are to lovingly accept them anyway. If they become somewhat abusive with their reaction, we are to try to endure and tolerate their response. This, indeed, is turning the other cheek. But then comes this other part of the passage, reminding us as we would have them do to us. We are not to be passive.

Stand Up for Christ

Jesus showed that there are also times when you need to stand up for what's right even if it offends others involved or the situation becomes necessarily aggressive or aversive. In Luke 11:37–54, Jesus was clearly confrontational with His Pharisee host. He didn't look the other way or ignore the situation. He went beyond defending Himself to exposing the ways of the Pharisees. He was not exactly winning friends and influencing people by His harsh, firm, and truthful words. In fact, He made some real enemies with His discourse. Jesus was not passive.

In Mark 7:1–23, Jesus again confronted the Pharisees. He admonished, ''You have a fine way of setting aside the commands of God in order to observe your own traditions'' (v. 9). He was saying that the Pharisees had developed their human regulations and believed them to be the way God would have them, even though they were far from what God desired. They were fooling themselves but not God.

We can be just as pharisaical as the Pharisees. Our motivations may seem to be the way God would have them, even though they may be at times far from what God desires. We can fool ourselves. We can read Scripture, memorize lengthy passages, understand theological teachings, attend legitimate church functions, and still miss the boat by not living and incorporating the truth of God's Word and will as He would have it. On the outside, it may look like the genuine thing, but to God, it's ''these people come near to me with their mouth and honor me with their lips, but their hearts are far from me'' (Isa. 29:13). The passive partner functionally does this, usually unknowingly, by distorting Christianity to allow the continuance of the passivity. The power partner functionally does this, usually unknowingly, to allow the continuance of the rigid life-style.

Jesus was not passive. In another, perhaps more well-known, situation, He took the initiative and drove out those who were selling in the temple area (see Matt. 21:12–13; Luke 19:45–46;

John 2:12–17). He overturned their tables and drove them out physically with a whip of cords.

Sometimes you must take tough stands.

Jesus' action at the temple really blows the passive partner's position. It also demonstrates that there are times when we should take tough stands—even with ourselves. Perhaps the toughest was at the Garden of Gethsemane. A passive Jesus would have said something like, "This cup is pretty tough! Isn't there some kind of Plan B? I'm outta here!" But Jesus was not passive: "My Father, if it is possible, may this cup be taken from me. Yet not as I will, but as you will" (Matt. 26:39). He went to the cross for you and me. He won victory over death, sin, and Satan. He also nailed passivity and rigidity to that cross, making it possible for His own to share in the completeness of His victory!

In forthcoming chapters, you'll get a better idea of balanced biblical Christianity and what it means for practical everyday living. First, though, you need a more precise understanding of the problem. Then you can work on changing it to a Christ-centered approach to life and relationships. The next chapter more specifically clarifies the passive partner concept.

Chapter 4

THE PASSIVE–DEPENDENT PARTNER UNVEILED

Joe Payne was a client who had come to see me for problems with chronic low back pain. It seemed that no treatment over the course of the past several years was able to provide any relief. Joe had been forced to retire early because the pain had become so debilitating that he could not function at his job. He felt continuous pain and discomfort, and his life-style had been greatly affected.

Joe's wife, Irma, told me that, prior to Joe's accident, their marriage wasn't doing very well, and Joe had seemed to be depressed quite often. It didn't take long to recognize that there were very real psychological factors involved in Joe's pain experience. Irma was the key to his eventual recovery.

Joe's physical pain had healed but was being perpetuated by operant pain processes. There were consequences to his pain experience that became instrumental in maintaining them. Prior to the accident, which began the entire pain experience, Joe was often ignored by Irma, who seemed to be so caught up with the details of her own everyday living that she wasn't very involved with Joe. After the accident, however, she became his twenty-four-hour nurse and caretaker. At first, it was irritating to Joe, but pretty soon it started to become a nice thing. He began to increasingly rely on her, and Irma felt a special sense of satisfaction, usefulness, and importance that she hadn't felt before. Similarly, Joe began to feel a special sense of appreciation, involvement, and value that he hadn't felt before. The actual physical pain became a secondary factor. Its real purpose was to allow continuation of the new relationship between Joe and Irma. It replaced their prior depression, isolation, and feelings of worthlessness.

I had to work with Irma to help her understand that she was reinforcing Joe's pain behavior by the special attention he was receiving from her. She had become an enabler in very much the same way the wife of an alcoholic begins to function. I explained that if an alcoholic came home inebriated, fell down on the floor, and passed out, his wife had two options. She could pick him up, put his pajamas on for him, and tuck him gently into bed, or she could leave him alone to suffer the consequences of his behavior. The former option made his alcoholic behavior seem less troublesome and distressing. Inwardly, the alcoholic might think, *This is bad——but not that bad. I think I'll have another drink!* His wife enabled him to continue the destructive behavior. The game plan needed to be changed.

The same principles applied to the continuation of Joe's chronic pain. Irma had to learn how *not* to enable and how *not* to reinforce the pain behaviors. She had become just as dependent on Joe as he had become dependent on her, and the codependency needed to stop so that recovery could occur. Joe needed tough love—not love that worked against him by reinforcing self-destructive and codependent behaviors. It took that kind of love for Christ to go to the cross. Christian love is patient but never passive.

To all appearances, Irma seemed to be a sacrificing individual who was doing the right thing and helping her husband. In reality, her sacrificing behaviors were more for her good than for her husband's recovery. Her behaviors reinforced his behaviors, and his responses reinforced her sacrificing behaviors. They had become codependent. Recovery involved helping both Joe and Irma recognize how their psychological needs were affecting Joe's physical condition. Irma's passive-dependency had allowed her to be an enabler to Joe's functional condition. Over the course of time, she had deteriorated into a wimp, and he had become a functional power person.

Such stories as that of Joe and Irma are not at all uncommon in the treatment of chronic pain processes, addictions, and a host of psychological problems. We gain insight also into how the passive-dependent person needs to learn to change for the good of self, for the good of the mate, and for the good of the relationship.

Passive-Dependency and Dewimping

In the previous chapter, we began to develop a working notion of the passive partner. The term *wimp* has been loosely and generally used to give a distasteful caricature of the extreme passive-dependent personality. This chapter describes the long-term features and personality characteristics of the passive (passive-dependent) partner. They are not given in any particular order. As with the rigid personality, there is some overlap for the characteristics of the passive partner.

As with the power partner, not every characteristic is necessary to make identification. However, the more features that apply, the worse the passivity. A minimum of two core characteristics is required to identify passivity. Any one descriptor is adequate to positively designate the entire trait (traits one through four). Remember that experiencing several of these criteria on an episodic basis is not enough to document real passive-dependency. Any person can wimp out on occasion. These characteristics represent a long-term, ongoing way of life.

The passive-dependent partner is

1. passive.
   - Waits for things to happen
   - Has problems being direct
   - Is fearful of taking a leadership role
   - Avoids conflict
2. others-oriented.
   - Is a pleaser; seeks approval
   - Is taken advantage of by others
   - Is unable to say no; is nonassertive
   - Is accepting of blame or responsibility even when it does not apply
   - Will tolerate emotional abuse
3. insecure.
   - Has low self-esteem
   - Lacks self-confidence
4. dependent.
   - Is indecisive
   - Is unsure
   - Is undemanding
   - Subordinates own needs to those of others
   - Fears abandonment; fears aloneness

1. The Passive Partner Is Unbiblically Passive

The passive partner usually does not initiate activities, events, relationships, or intimacy. For the most part, the passive partner is a responder who waits for things to happen. The passive partner may also be fearful of taking a leadership role. The passive partner tries to avoid relational conflict.

Molly and George Carter had come for marital therapy. A passive-dependent personality had married a rigid personality. These two personality types attract each other and seem to seek each other out. George and Molly had fallen prey to the arousing allure of each other's psychopathology when they dated and were first married, but now that appeal was waning. And the marital imbalance and dissatisfaction were taking a toll on

Molly. George was more upset because Molly was uncooperative at home and in their relationship. Molly was burned out with their relationship. She was depressed and confused. He simply wanted her "fixed."

When I asked Molly what had originally attracted her to George, she quickly answered that he seemed to be a leader, confident of what he wanted out of life. He had pursued her in their relationship. Molly felt flattered and secure in George's apparent interest and leadership.

Had George not initiated things relationally with Molly, she wouldn't have had a relationship with him. She most likely wouldn't have had any relationships had no one else taken the lead. But Molly let George lead. His lead turned into domination. But Molly didn't find that out until after marriage.

Such is the plight of the passive-dependent person. Unfortunately, the Christian community, in a genuine effort to follow God's Word, often misses the dilemma of such a relationship, confusing spiritual leadership and the priestly role of the husband with permission for emotional and psychological domination and abuse. The passive partner gets branded the bad guy for trying to obtain respect and mutual submission. Subsequently, the passive partner withdraws and gives up the hope of mutual respect and mutual submission. The passive partner may also give up on the Christian community and sometimes may give up on Christ.

2. The Passive Partner Is Others-Oriented

The inability to appropriately care for self in order to take care of others' needs is the trademark of the passive partner. The passive partner has trouble in almost every interpersonal situation and is no match for the rigid personality. The passive partner is others-oriented. The passive partner is a pleaser who seeks approval. In comparison to significant others, the passive partner has no place of importance, constantly allowing others this emotional seat of honor.

At first, this may sound like the biblical thing to do, but such action by the passive partner is not based on Scripture or a love for the Lord. Rather, it is based on the individual's personality and related emotional needs. Like so many other characteristics that seem godly, this distinctive is self-centered rather than Christ-centered. The underlying rationale for such behavior is self-protection of the passive partner's tender ego state. Additionally, it's just easier and allows conflict avoidance.

It's OK to say no.

The passive partner is unable to say no. If the passive partner attempts to be assertive, the other person doesn't really believe such assertiveness is genuine and challenges the behavior. Because the passive partner seeks to avoid conflict, the challenge usually ends up with the passive partner giving in.

This kind of others-orientation is not Christ-centered. Though it looks like "the real McCoy," it is more like a Christian decoy. Though there is the appearance of Christian goodness, the motivation is wrong. Many passive partners rationalize their behavior as valid Christian submission, servitude, or martyrdom. Passive partners are obviously capable of valid Christian service and do perform many acts of Christian goodness. However, specific acts of Christian kindness should not be confused with the broader life-style and self-serving pattern of passive partners.

Adler believed that all behavior is purposeful. There are psychological purposes for wimp behavior. The others-oriented partner wants to be accepted, fears rejection, needs approval, wants to avoid conflict (perceiving conflict to be a type of rejection), and/or wants to please others (in order to feel accepted). A life-style develops to allow pursuance of these deeper psychological, egocentric needs. As with the power partner, these needs are usually beyond the passive partner's awareness.

Molly Carter was others-oriented. George didn't mind that at all—as long as he was the "other." However, if Molly's others-orientation involved people besides George, he found that to be most unacceptable.

Molly would often wind up in double jeopardy. Her peers would take advantage of her, then George would resent her for it (a double whammy)! And it seemed that everyone knew Molly was a soft touch. Others constantly sought her out to do things for them. If no one else was willing to do a job, they could always turn to Molly.

In social situations as well as at home, Molly would often take the blame for something, even when it clearly was not her fault. On one occasion, she asked George to accompany her to visit a close friend with whom there had been a misunderstanding that day. Prior to leaving, George coached her in exactly what to say. Molly's friend was clearly in the wrong. She also was obviously taking advantage of Molly in the situation.

George escorted Molly to her friend's home. He watched from an adjacent room as Molly boldly and confidently walked right up to her friend, looked her in the eye, cocked her head forward, and said, "I'm sorry for what happened today. It was all my fault. Please forgive me." Before her friend could respond, George dropped his iced tea in his lap in disbelief and dismay. Though it was okay for Molly to wimp out with him, it was very annoying that she did it with others. Molly was quick to clean up George's spilled drink and to bring him another.

Later that night at home, George exploded into a tirade. He called Molly to task for wimping out and for embarrassing him. But Molly was used to such an emotional affront. It had happened many times before in various forms. She endured it outwardly, though inwardly she was crushed and dispirited.

Molly has helped us get a feel for the others-oriented partner. Of course, her pattern is flagrant and easily identifiable. Many times this same pattern exists but occurs less often and less predictably, and it is much more subtle and less readily discernible—especially to the passive partner.

3. The Passive Partner Is Insecure

Underneath the outer facade and external behavior, the passive partner shares a common core characteristic with the power partner: both are basically insecure individuals possessing low self-esteem and having poor self-confidence. The exterior of the passive partner may appear unaffected and remote. The exterior of the power partner may appear formidable and threatening. The appearance of each is a cover-up for an underlying ego deficit.

Mark McMann, a passive partner, gave the appearance of a humble, meek, submissive, self-controlled individual who was known for leading a popular Bible study in his church. In actuality, he moderated a highly structured class, which was taught via video and textbooks from a pop Christian figure and organization. Passive partners and power partners are attracted to such courses of study.

Behind closed counseling office doors, Mark confided deep distress and dissatisfaction with himself and with his Christian walk. He feared any conflict and never spoke up for his viewpoints. Rather, he went along with whatever other Christians said. Even if he disagreed with other believers, he would give in to their viewpoints to keep peace and avoid conflict.

Such behaviors gave the appearance of being humble, meek, and submissive. Inwardly, Mark resented those other Christians for always getting their way. Yet he appeared unaffected. Mark recognized that he sought approval at all costs—even at the cost of forfeiting his views and rights. He greatly feared disapproval and rejection. Subsequently, he always let others have their way. He would give input, but he would back off if there was any hint of conflict brewing. His response looked like submission and meekness, but it was old-fashioned wimping out. He looked like he was very self-controlled, but he had no self-confidence. He felt insecure.

Due to his insecurity, he missed out on much of the richness of the Christian life. He also was disobedient. Christianity is always a balanced life. Sometimes we are to be submissive.

Sometimes we are to be discriminating. Sometimes we are to be confrontational. Mark could do the first one well, but he could not do the latter ones.

Mark was also distraught about his inability to take stands that were unpopular with non-Christians. He wimped out in those situations, too. Yet Christians are to be lights to the world and salt to the earth (see Matt. 5:13–16). Christians are to expect the world to hate Jesus in us the way the world hated Jesus when He was in the world (see John 15:19). Christianity is not a popularity contest; it will meet with resistance, disapproval, rejection, and even hate. We cannot be wholly approved by the world and be approved as holy by God. Such is the practical dilemma, as Mark subjectively experienced, of the insecure passive partner.

4. The Passive Partner Is Dependent

The passive partner is dependent. This characteristic is closely related to the others-oriented characteristic, and it may be another way of looking at the same thing. However, the others-oriented characteristic is an active one whereas the dependent characteristic is a passive one. Most important, the passive partner fears emotional and psychological abandonment by significant others (usually the rigid personality). Such emotional withdrawal elicits the fear of aloneness. This fear of emotional abandonment, helplessness, and loneliness is unbearable to the dependent personality.

The others-oriented partner looks to others for immediate approval and acceptance. The feedback is quickly discernible. The dependent partner is more subtle and not as readily perceptive of feedback. Being unsure of the feedback, the dependent partner hesitates and becomes indecisive. Going forward with a decision requires some guarantee that, at worst, all is safe and, at best, others (especially the power partner) will be agreeable to the choice—as if it were their choice and the dependent partner was an extension of them in the decision-making process. The dependent partner passively subordinates personal needs to the needs of others. And those needs can be actual needs or demands or the passive partner's perception of others' needs or demands.

Kirk and Lee Anne Poston had been married twenty-five years. Kirk was a classic power partner, and Lee Anne was a classic passive partner. Kirk spent a lot of time debuilding. By debuilding, I mean the opposite of building up. He undermined Lee Anne's confidence in herself and continually criticized her.

Kirk's debuilding was almost an art. He was very good at it. He balanced it with some occasional encouragement and positive attention, especially when Lee Anne focused exclusively on him, but he knew how to keep her doubting herself enough so that her self-concept was virtually nonexistent. It was not a deliberate, methodical, well-thought-out plan; rather, it was a style of relating. Kirk was killing two birds with one stone. Debuilding discouraged Lee Anne and adversely affected her self-concept, and it made Kirk feel superior. Emotionally, putting her down lifted him up.

Of course, in the long run, such treatment was mutually self-destructive. But like a drug addict, Kirk didn't look beyond his next fix. Psychology textbooks call it the *neurotic paradox*— the psychological pattern is working, even though it is harmful. And the person(s) caught up in the pattern can't see the harm or alternatives, so the ruinous cycle continues.

Lee Anne was afraid of emotional abandonment, helplessness, loneliness, and aloneness. Because of her deep fears, she adopted the outlook that she would try to do everything she could to ensure that Kirk never emotionally abandoned her. You don't have to physically leave to emotionally depart. Whenever Lee Anne perceived any distance in her relationship with Kirk, she eventually gave in to his demands, however unreasonable they were. He kept her dependent, and he took advantage of her fears and dependency. He used her dependency as a manipulative tool to get his way. No matter what else occurred between them, no matter how Lee Anne outmaneuvered him, or outwitted him, or outdid him, Kirk held the trump card. And he knew he did. He wasn't afraid to use it. And he felt superior because of that leverage.

Kirk really didn't need to play his trump card very often. Lee Anne was keenly aware of her dependency, and sometimes she perceived that emotional abandonment was forthcoming even if Kirk had not considered it. She did a lot of his dirty work for him, without his knowledge, but he got the full credit. Her fears and anxiety kept her in an emotionally oppressed condition.

Kirk and Lee Anne demonstrate how the characteristics of the power partner and the passive partner work together. Feeding off each other, they coexist in a cancerous relationship.

The passive partner is passive and/or others-oriented and/or insecure and/or dependent. The above descriptors and explanations present a severe case of passive-dependency. However, it takes only one descriptor or elaboration to qualify. Two core characteristics denote positive identification of the passive partner.

In the next chapter we will further examine how characteristics of both personality types operate together. We have looked at the individual personalities, and now we turn our attention to understanding the dysfunctional pattern of the relationship.

Chapter 5

THE RELATIONSHIP'S IMPACT ON THE MARRIAGE

"It's all my fault. He's right. I'm the reason those roaches got into the kitchen."

"I beg your pardon?"

"Rich [her husband] was right. I shouldn't have told him about those roaches. I told him I had seen one, so we needed to wash all the utensils where it had been. He exploded. Yelled at me! He said it was my fault. I should have been able to do something."

"Do what?"

"I don't know. I told him last week we had roaches. He never did anything about it. He told me it was my problem, so I put down paper and sprayed. I guess it is my fault."

"Are you saying the roaches were there because of you?"

"Yes. Rich was right. It's my fault. And I shouldn't have bothered him."

"I'm still not clear as to how it was your fault. What do you mean?"

"It's because of me. He's right."

"Do you think you have some special influence or something?"

"I don't know."

"Should I just refer to you as the bug lady? You put the paper down . . . you sprayed . . . it must be you . . . they're attracted to you! But if that's the case, why don't you just stand outside? Let them follow you out of the kitchen. Maybe you could lead them down to the river, stand knee deep, and drown them all."

"That's silly." (*Laughs.*)

"You could start an exterminating business . . . the Pied Piper of Pests . . . and Rich could be your manager . . . or agent . . . since he was the one to recognize this incredible ability you have."

"When you put it like that, it does sound ridiculous . . . absurd."

This conversation actually occurred in a counseling session. I didn't want to believe it, either. But when you stop to think about it, it's not that surprising.

Recall that one characteristic of the rigid personality is that he cannot accept responsibility so he blames others for whatever unacceptable event happens. Recall that one characteristic of the passive-dependent personality is that she is others-oriented and will accept blame even when it does not apply. Put the two characteristics operating together, and you've got one person perpetually punting and the other person perpetually receiving. This process becomes a habit and develops into a couple's way of relating, a life-style, a game.

It is not so surprising, then, that Sheila believed the far-out story that she was to blame for having roaches in the kitchen. It was an automatic response without much thinking taking place. Since Rich always blamed her for things that went wrong, and since she always accepted responsibility for things that went wrong (though she didn't quite understand how), she accepted Rich's accusations one more time.

Add to this the knowledge that the passive partner seeks to avoid conflict and wants to please others. Also add to this the knowledge that the power partner can be intimidating and authoritative. These qualities applied to Sheila and Rich. We could expect something like this in any power-passive relationship.

The Illusion of Safety

In a power-passive relationship, or marriage, a rigid personality has become emotionally and psychologically connected to a passive-dependent personality and vice versa. They are codependent. Each needs the other and becomes emotionally dependent on the relationship's remaining the same. The payoff is that it allows the false feelings of security, safety, and success that the neurotic paradox deceptively feeds.

The previous chapters have discussed individual characteristics of the power partner and the passive partner. Rich and Sheila demonstrate that the power partner and the passive partner are uniquely suited for each other. They naturally meet each other's emotional and psychological needs. Unfortunately, these are not healthy psychological needs. Such relationships are time bombs. The extent of the explosion depends on the extent of rigidity and passivity, individually and relationally.

Rich and Sheila are Christians. One of the most diabolical deceptions around is that all Christians have their acts together, and that simply being a Christian guarantees automatic happiness and bliss. If you don't have perpetual gladness, you really aren't a Christian anyway. Or you aren't Spirit-filled. Or you need to "up" your faith. Or at the very least, you have backslidden. Any way you consider it, you are a disgrace!

Good Christians have problems.

But none of this is true. All Christians don't have their acts together. Many, if not most, don't. Does that mean they really aren't Christians? Not at all. Does that mean they have backslidden? Maybe. But more likely it is something else. Even we Christians sometimes don't really appreciate or recognize the full effects and seriousness of sin and of the fall of humankind. Christians have problems. We have unique blind spots, which prevent us from adequately seeing our problems. The power partner and the passive partner have such blind spots. Both justify their behavior as purely biblical, yet, much, if not most, of the time, it is not.

The more severe the pattern of rigidity or passivity, the more likely there exists extrabiblical motivation for behavior. By extrabiblical, I mean beyond a biblical explanation: if such behavior meets the criteria of biblical mandate—fine and well and preferable—but the heart motivation is not, at the foundational level, based on the biblical directive. Proverbs 21:2 tells us, ''All a man's ways seem right to him, but the LORD weighs the heart.'' Just because our ways seem right to us or feel righteous doesn't mean they are necessarily right.

These hard teachings are not intended to frighten, frustrate, or confuse us. Rather, we, as Christians, are challenged to examine ourselves to pursue holiness (see Ps. 139:23–24; 2 Cor. 13:5).

Rich and Sheila were Christians, but their patterns of behavior, individually and relationally, were not always Christlike. Though it was obvious in the opening example, it is not always so apparent. For example, had Rich exploded inwardly, it would have seemed much less offensive but would have been just as wrong. Rather than yell and use abusive speech, he could have abusively pouted, sulked, and/or refused to talk. This is passive-aggressive behavior, but it is just as poisonous as the assaultive tirade. At other times such behavior is even more subtle and goes unnoticed by all but Christ.

A related deception is that a genuine conversion experience completely changes everything within that person. As a general rule, the basic personality doesn't completely change when someone becomes a Christian. The spiritual pneumonia may seem to go away but, more often, will appear as a milder version of itself, such as a runny nose. But the essence and basic propensity are the same.

The potential to overcome negative components of that personality changes, but the personality itself doesn't go away. Though it often doesn't manifest itself the way it formerly did, the potential to do so remains. It may be helpful to think of the destructive aspect of the personality as being in remission. It's not as evident or overtly bothersome as before, but there is the capability of returning to a full-blown malignancy.

The believer often encounters a battle of spiritual and fleshly dimensions. Romans 7:14—8:17 describes such a battle by the apostle Paul. This battle seems to be a part of the Christian walk. Yet for the power partner and the passive partner, much of this battle is being fought blindfolded. And too much of the time, the battle is one-sided in that neither the rigid nor the passive personality is adequately aware of the full impact or effect of the battle. Though the person feels the wound, there is no sight of artillery; there is no smell of gunsmoke; there is no sound of gunfire.

Codependent Deception

Rich and Sheila are codependent. They are addicted to each other. Their unconscious psychological need is to stay codependent, so they do. Their biblical directive is quite different. Scripture teaches us to become increasingly dependent on Christ's sufficiency alone. Rich's job is to help Sheila do that. Sheila's job is to help Rich do that. Yet both remain codependent rather than Christ-dependent. Neither is aware of the fuller extent of the dilemma.

Does this type of power-passive relationship affect only Christians? Not at all. But this book is directed to Christians because we are more likely to be uniquely blindsided by such personalities and relationships. We fool ourselves into believing that such things don't really exist, especially for Christians. If they do, the individuals involved can't really be born again or Spirit-filled. That is not necessarily so.

We can also fool ourselves into believing that, if some of these symptoms exist in our lives, they really are genuinely spiritual and Christ-centered. Perhaps they are virtues. Not so. The heart determines such things, and the mind hides their negative motivation. Our flesh distorts the truth of our hidden motives. There is also spiritual warfare, and we are being deceived. All of this isn't happening all the time, but even if it's happening only some of the time, it is still wrong. It is still sin. And this blocks growth in Christ.

Ask others to help you see yourself.

A word of caution is appropriate here. We should not rely on our own ability to assess ourselves. Certainly, we should not eliminate ourselves entirely from the evaluation process, but we must recognize that our views of ourselves may be tainted—for better or worse—but off the mark either way. We should ask other trusted Christians to provide their truthful feedback. Such trusted Christians may be, but are not limited to, spouses, family members, brothers and sisters in Christ, or church leaders. It may take the skills of a well-trained Christian counselor to see behind the veil.

Power partners and passive partners seldom see themselves accurately. As far as they are concerned, all is well, thank you. But if you can get just below the surface, there is a good chance some truth may come out.

If you can see some of these characteristics in yourself, or if you can see some of these processes in your marriage, there is real hope for you. You have overcome the first barrier of denial, and your new awareness possesses the ability to guide you to victory. A good hard-core power partner would find some way to dismiss such a self-examination or relational investigation. A good soft-core passive partner would let that happen. If you, or your mate, are open to the recognition of some of these traits or patterns in your life, the first step toward healing has already begun.

Differentiation Assassination

Just as there are identifying marks of each personality, there are identifiable patterns for a power-passive relationship. It isn't likely that any one relationship will have every one of the patterns described in this chapter, but it is certainly possible. It is more likely that a few may be there. None of these patterns is good for any relationship.

Perhaps the hallmark pattern, and the most perpetuating and self-destructive one, is the one I would term *differentiation assassination*. Differentiation assassination occurs when the passive partner starts to go against the grain of the passivity, but before the person's self-confidence has any chance to gain momentum, all efforts and progress are sabotaged either by the passive partner or, more likely, by the power partner. The passive partner is blocked from differentiating and turned back toward the former relational pattern.

Debbie Dent realized the extreme control her husband, Todd, exerted over her, and she was pleased with her ability to try to break the destructive cycle of their marriage. By becoming less dependent on Todd, Debbie reasoned that she would be able to break the silent yoke of domination she felt. She realized that it was a good thing for Todd as well.

Debbie went into real estate and very quickly became a top salesperson. She was pleasantly surprised by her success. Unfortunately, the more successful Debbie became, the more upset Todd became. Todd emotionally realized that their codependent relationship was in great danger. Though he didn't fully understand what was happening, his instinct sounded the alarm loudly.

Rather than be encouraging and positive about Debbie's success, Todd made statements to make her feel badly and discouraged. It was not a well-thought-out process but an unconscious, instinctive, and spontaneous way of relating to her. For example, he would focus on her time spent away from home, implying that she was not being a biblical or responsible wife (even though she was more "at home" and available than Todd).

This behavior is an example of another set of rules for relationships established by a power partner: (1) I make the rules; (2) you must obey the rules; (3) I am exempt from the rules; and (4) if you don't cooperate, I'll find ways to punish you or make you feel badly.

On one occasion, Debbie tried earnestly to show her devotion to Todd and their home by redecorating their den and bedroom. Though Todd agreed to the original plan, he complained and criticized every piece of furniture or decor that Debbie proposed. He always found something wrong, and Debbie's confidence in her decorating abilities, and in herself, plummeted.

Eventually, Debbie overcame Todd's negativity and criticism. She felt herself gaining self-confidence. She learned not to let his criticism affect her to the depths it previously had. But Todd exercised the ultimate threat: he was going to leave Debbie if she didn't straighten up and return to being the submissive wife. He argued that he had always treated her nicely. He further argued that she really had nothing to complain about. The Christian community certainly would side with him.

He told her that he had consulted with an attorney about his legal rights for separation—not that he really wanted to do that. Debbie wasn't as ready as she thought she was. The timing was bad. Rather than become increasingly Christ-dependent, due to her dependency needs and her fear of abandonment, Debbie wimped out and went immediately back into the codependent role. Shortly thereafter, she resigned from her real estate job. A few months later, she came to me for professional help for her depression.

Such is one pattern of the power-passive relationship. It is a very difficult pattern to break. In this chapter we have already seen some of the dynamics of the power-passive relationship. The power partner can be a blamer. The passive partner accepts unnecessary blame. The power partner can be controlling and demanding. The passive partner avoids conflict and seeks to please others, subordinating personal needs to others (for unbiblical reasons). The power partner can be authoritative. The passive partner wants someone else to lead. The power partner can be intimidating and may try to make significant others feel inferior or inadequate. The passive partner is dependent, feels inadequate, and fears abandonment.

So far it doesn't look too good for the passive partner. The passive partner seems to constantly lose, and the power partner seems to constantly win. In reality, both lose.

Power-Passive Patterns

Another relational dynamic can be the self-focusing characteristic of the power partner versus the others-oriented characteristic of the passive partner. The power partner may appear to be acting biblically but, many times, is just taking care of number one and using Christianity as a vehicle to do that: "submit so that I can have my way" versus "let's both submit to Christ and each other so that Christ can have His way."

The power partner can be selfish. The passive partner is self-giving. Both are that way for the wrong reasons. The passive partner loses out in two ways. First, the power partner gets to indulge self again, and second, the passive partner's behavior, though it looks biblical outwardly, is not biblical. This is not self-giving in the sense of putting on Christ. It is self-giving in the sense of protecting one's needs and preserving the codependent relationship.

The power partner can be stubborn, unable to be reasoned with, and inflexible. The passive partner is often indecisive and gives in to whatever the power partner demands.

The power partner can be empathy-impaired. The passive partner tolerates emotional neglect and abuse. Even in extreme cases where there is the threat of physical abuse or cruel emotional abuse, the passive partner allows continuance of this threat by passive tolerance of such actions and a fear of initiating self-protective change. Such tolerance may be attributed to a denial of reality, to a love and deeper understanding of the mate than others would understand, or to a feeling of suffering for Christ. But though such rationalizations may give comfort in affliction, the passive-dependent soul is blindly chained to codependency.

The power partner can distort the world by seeing only in extremes. Issues are viewed as being either all right or all wrong. There is no give-and-take, no ability to negotiate, and no ability to compromise. The passive partner is unable to say no and is easily taken advantage of.

The power partner can be self-focused sexually and seek only personal pleasure. The spouse is there for the power partner's needs rather than both giving of themselves, in love, to each other.

The passive partner can be insecure and have low self-confidence. The power partner, though insecure at a deep level, appears externally confident and self-assured. The passive partner is attracted to the power partner's apparent confidence, hoping to compensate for a lack of self-confidence. Trouble arises later when the real nature of the power partner surfaces. But the fact of insecurity seldom arises. It's bad for the image. Often, there is intense emotional energy indicating dissatisfaction in a general sense rather than recognizing or admitting the power partner's fears.

Of course, the passive partner is quick to accept responsibility, even when it does not apply, to keep the peace. Much of the time the passive partner doesn't completely realize what is occurring, noting instead strong feelings and behaviors by the power partner but not fully understanding them. The passive partner needs to see the power partner as strong and secure, so the passive partner maintains the illusion of self-confidence and psychological muscle. Yet the power partner may be the weaker of the two. The passive partner feels confused because of the relational razzle-dazzle unconsciously designed to keep the heat off the power partner while registering emotional discontent. Any self-confidence is thereby undermined and stripped away. This sort of thing occurred in the incident with Rich and Sheila.

The power partner can be jealous and insecure. The power partner will spend money and time on the self or the career but will sternly resist the passive partner's doing the same thing. Often, the power partner won't let the spouse develop friendships outside the home. They can be too threatening—even if such friendships are family or church oriented. It is not necessarily done directly. Many times the power partner gives nonverbal signs of disapproval, such as pouting or being angry and resentful. The passive partner gets the message. Before too long, the passive partner learns that it is easier to let the power partner win. Outside support systems are abandoned. Self-confidence teeters on the edge of brokenness and defeat. And the codependent dynamic intensifies and hardens.

This chapter has focused on descriptive dynamics within the power-passive relationship. Again, not every power-passive relationship has every theme. The more themes that are recognized within a relationship, however, the more dysfunctional the relationship. It is possible to have all of the themes. Though we have hit on the main themes, there are many variations and degrees of each one.

For example, the theme of controller-pleaser can range from extremely rigid and dysfunctional to mildly rigid and problematic. The appearance of the relationship is not the determining factor anyway. Rather, it is that unspoken working understanding and perception of each of its members. In one relationship, it may take a raised voice and a threat of physical or emotional harm to clearly send a restrictive message to a mate; in another relationship, a look or an understanding will accomplish the same thing. Both operate under the same rules. Both are dysfunctional.

Characteristics of the Power-Passive Relationship

These themes seem to run through the fabric of the power-passive relationship:

- Controller-pleaser
- Authoritarian-follower
- Blamer-accepter of fault
- Demanding-undemanding
- Self-focused–others-oriented
- Assassinator-differentiator
- Independent-dependent
- Deserter-deserted one
- Intimidator-inferior
- Decisive-indecisive
- Extremist-assenter
- Defensive-conciliatory

All of these dynamics are dysfunctional. One to three of these characteristics in a relationship suggest mild dysfunction. Four to six suggest moderate, or mid-range, dysfunction. Seven or more of these relational characteristics suggest severe dysfunction. The problems and effects of the relationship may not be obvious to outside observers, or even to the power or passive partners, but they negatively affect the relationship, especially the passive-dependent member. The impact can range from recognized dissatisfaction to unrecognized, internalized depression or psychophysiological complaints.

There is also a range of behaviors for each relational characteristic. The degree varies from couple to couple and is unique to each relationship. The couple may vary on characteristics and/or vary on the range, features, and levels of any characteristic. Obviously, the more characteristics that you find in your relationship, the more self-destructive your relationship. Similarly, the more features or levels of a particular characteristic, the more self-defeating the characteristic. It takes only a minimal level to completely qualify on a feature.

Some couples may recognize some of these characteristics as being in their past. That's a good start. But you should honestly check to see if there are remaining characteristics or hidden ones in the present. This pattern doesn't go away overnight. It will take awareness and hard, continual work to overcome the destructiveness. The last part of this chapter briefly reviews these characteristics to clarify their meaning and to give some idea of the range within each characteristic. You also may want to review sections of chapters 2 and 4 defining power and passive-dependent partners.

A Controller-Pleaser Relationship

In the severely rigid controller-pleaser relationship, rules of operation are very restrictive, and the power partner takes away almost all freedom from the mate. Such loss of freedom may include, but is not limited to, issues and decisions about money, time, work, and family. Most, if not all, of life's decisions are centered on the power partner's choices and wants. The pleaser gives in to the rigid controller.

Ken and Wendy Trollins (in chapter 2) typified the severely rigid controller-pleaser relationship with their way of money management. Ken virtually controlled all money. He allowed Wendy to put her income into the family pot. Ken would pay all the bills, make major purchases, and give Wendy an allowance. She had no idea how much money was in the family pot, nor did she have any idea of Ken's income. He had charge cards, for emergency use, but she had none. He made large purchases, which he thought of benefit to his career. Her career was unimportant; therefore, there was no need to invest any money in it. After all, he argued, a biblical wife's place was in the home.

Though Ken and Wendy's situation is presented as severe in terms of money management, other situations may be worse! We looked at only one subcategory of the controller-pleaser relationship. The important thing to remember is that there is a loss of freedom, and perhaps an accompanying loss of dignity, for this type of characteristic in a relationship. The worse this characteristic, the more the loss of freedom and dignity for every subcategory.

Pleasers lose freedom to controllers.

For the sake of illustration, let's assume that Ken and Wendy's situation represented the severe end of the continuum. The moderate range might include the rigid husband who closely monitors all moneys coming in and going out, and who subtly lets his mate know of his displeasure without being so overtly tight. The passive partner is involved in the sense that she knows how much money she can spend. The moderate and mild range would include the husband who won't allow his mate respect and freedom, coupled with responsibility and good stewardship, with household moneys. In the mild range, the controller-husband may allow the pleaser-wife total control over budgeted expenditures, but he has to keep a close watch to be sure the best buys are obtained. He may not say too much, remaining subtly influential, but the pleaser-wife knows he is looking over her shoulder and she'd better make him happy.

An Authoritarian–Follower Relationship

Ron and Patsy Rodman (in chapter 1) illustrated the authoritarian-follower characteristic of the power-passive relationship. Ron was the authoritarian. There is a difference between an authoritarian and an authority. The latter has credence; the former has none but has definite personality needs. It becomes confusing when, as in Ron's situation, there is some special training, knowledge, or experience that lends an air of authority to the situation. In Ron's case, his seminary training and personal knowledge of Scripture seemed to give his perspective of his marital problems a resonance of authority. But when we looked deep below the surface, we discovered it served as a smoke screen to get his way.

Ron represents the severely rigid authoritarian. He misused his "authority" to virtually dictate judgments to his wife, Patsy, who felt something was wrong but quietly assented to Ron's supremacy. The severely rigid authoritarian is always the final say about everything (in his opinion), and the follower trusts his judgments. Unfortunately, she often is so overshadowed by his influence that she is deprived of the chance to take leadership and make judgments of her own. Later, she wonders why her self-confidence is so poor. Because of her poor self-confidence, she leans more on her authoritarian husband, and their destructive cycle continues in a downward spiral. This process helps explain how a mild authoritarian-follower relationship can degenerate into a severe one.

Like all the characteristics, the authoritarian-follower characteristic is unique to each relationship in terms of the range of associated behaviors. The range would depend on the degree and stuckness of the authoritarianism. The severe authoritarian has already been described. The mid-range, or moderate, authoritarian would be less confident and determined about authority. The moderate authoritarian would use authority less than the severe authoritarian, who constantly uses it. The moderate authoritarian would appear insistent and dogmatic about an issue but would not be so forcefully and adamantly assured. The mild authoritarian would seek to minimally include others' opinions before issuing a proclamation. The frequency of authoritarian behavior would be much less evident, being primarily concerned about major issues of the week. The severe authoritarian makes every issue a major issue of the day. The mild authoritarian would allow the spouse to have limited input when making a judgment about a novel situation.

A Blamer-Accepter Relationship

The severely rigid personality who is a blamer cannot take responsibility for anything. One characteristic of the passive dependent personality is the ability to accept blame even when it's not the person's fault. At the beginning of this chapter, Rich and Sheila demonstrated how far and outlandish this relational dynamic can go. Rich blamed Sheila for having roaches in the kitchen, and Sheila believed him! Doesn't that just bug you, too?

This dynamic is more often considered to be the wooden leg syndrome by psychologists. The argument goes something like this: "If it weren't for this wooden leg, then . . ." The implication is that the person would then accomplish something that was presently unable to be achieved. The moderately rigid blamer sings this song with the accepter playing the role of the wooden leg. The accepter often believes that the wooden leg role is legitimate. At other times, the accepter takes responsibility because it is the practical thing to do, avoiding conflict and simultaneously placating the mate.

Rich and Sheila reflect the severe level of this blamer-accepter dynamic. At such a level, the rigid blamer perpetually blames the accepter for all problems, shortcomings, and frustrations. At the moderate level, the accepter is concerned about holding back the mate, who tolerates the accepter's ineptitude. Blaming occurs for major difficulties in the relationship but not for everything wrong with their life together. At the mild level, there is far less blaming, though it certainly continues, perhaps at an implied level, and both mates have learned to work around the accepter's shortcomings and perpetual blunders. The accepter is often accommodated by being viewed as spacey but well-intentioned.

A Demanding-Undemanding Relationship

The power partner can be very demanding and impatient. The passive partner can be undemanding and dependent. By combining these two personal characteristics into a relational characteristic, a dynamic evolves with one person making all the demands and the other trying to fix things.

The main feature of this relational characteristic is the power partner's demandingness. It can range from severely demanding (perpetual ventilation of complaints and subsequent demands that things be immediately repaired) to mildly demanding (occasional grumbling with implied expectation for the satisfier to take care of the matter).

A Self-Focused–Others-Oriented Relationship

It's easy to tell if the power-passive couple possesses this dynamic, but it's hard to talk about it. It will immediately show up in the couple's sex life. The power partner is interested in fulfilling his sexual needs by using his wife's body and sexual behaviors he feels appropriate. Romantic love, thoughtfulness, tenderness, and consideration of his wife are lacking. Oh, there's a certain amount of consideration—after all, he wants her to show up, and he expects her to perform. But it's a one-way street. He reminds his wife that she is to "do unto others" and further clarifies that he is the "others" they are talking about!

The severely self-focused personality will roll over and surprise his wife even if she's in a dead sleep. And if she doesn't wake up, the surprise party keeps right on going anyway! The moderately self-focused personality wants his mate to enjoy sex, but it's more a matter of wanting her to enjoy making love to him than it is a matter of enjoying his lovemaking. The mildly self-focused personality hopes his wife has a good time, but if she doesn't, that's just too bad.

These comments have been confined to sexual functioning, but the self-focus described for this relational dynamic extends to every area of life. The self-focused personality's theme song is the Frank Sinatra rendition of "I Did It My Way." The second favorite song is the Beatles' "I Me Mine."

An Assassinator-Differentiator Relationship

This dynamic was illustrated by Todd and Debbie Dent. Debbie tried to do what every passive-dependent partner should attempt to do. She tried to differentiate, to go against the grain of the codependent pattern established with her partner. The goal should be to become totally Christ-dependent and to break out of the codependent, passive-dependent role. No one can be Christ-dependent and relationally codependent.

Codependency is usually learned from one's family of origin, and it is a characteristic found in dysfunctional families. This same codependency functioning is applied to the power-passive relationship. Though this book focuses on the codependency of the marital relationship, this same codependency can evolve throughout the entire family. Many times, if not most times, the couples I see for this power-passive relational pattern also have the same pattern affecting their larger family.

Breaking out of this codependent relational pattern is hard enough with mutual cooperation and understanding between the codependent partners. It is almost impossible to accomplish with the passive-dependent personality alone and nearly as impossible for the power personality alone. The ideal setting for change includes two cooperative, understanding, and determined partners plus a well-trained and highly skilled therapist. It can minimally be done with one member of the relationship plus the therapist (or caring, trained helper). In any event, such change requires a long, tough process. With Christ's help, change can be accomplished if one or both partners will persevere.

The assassinator-differentiator dynamic refers to the process of one partner (the differentiator) trying to break out of the dysfunctional, codependent role while the other partner (the assassinator) continually threatens and sabotages the attempts. Even when both partners try to be consciously cooperative, one or both may unconsciously assume the assassinator role. This process is similar to the neurotic paradox discussed previously as applied to an individual. Here the neurotic paradox applies to the relationship. Even though it is self-destructive for the relationship to continue as it is, the relationship will try to remain the same.

An Independent-Dependent Relationship

This relational dynamic is easily understood in the context of the previous one. Due to the codependent situation, both partners actually depend on each other. In practice, though, the power personality appears independent. The power partner tries to believe in personal independence and tries to convince others, especially the passive-dependent partner, of it. The more doubtful and insecure the power partner feels about self and

Power partners are dependent, too.

independence (and though they are not consciously recognized, below the outer facade of certainty and autonomy, there certainly are doubt and insecurity), the more effort the power partner will put into building up the external appearance of self-sufficiency and competency. Conversely, the passive partner is usually not as dependent on the power partner as is felt or believed.

A Deserter-Deserted One Relationship

This relational dynamic is closely connected to the previous one. The power partner knows that the passive-dependent partner fears abandonment and aloneness. Therefore, the power partner uses the appearance of independence as a threat to the passive partner's fears to intimidate and to manipulate the passive partner. This expressed or unexpressed threat gives power to the rigid personality and increases false feelings of self-worth.

An Intimidator-Inferior Relationship

This dynamic is similar to the previous one in that power and increased ego are gained for the power partner. The power partner frightens and discourages the passive-dependent partner. These fear tactics are not necessarily direct or apparent. Already feeling insecure and wanting to please others, especially the rigid mate, the passive partner is easily intimidated.

The intimidation varies but usually contains some form of the message "you cannot function or succeed adequately without my help." Because of the authoritarian characteristic, the power partner is considered to be the valid judge of whatever effort is being attempted by the passive partner, who concedes to whatever determination is reached. Such a power position by the rigid personality keeps the passive-dependent personality in a perpetual one-down position, reinforcing feelings of inadequacy. Again, due to the codependent nature of the relationship, should the passive-dependent personality show signs of success in an endeavor, the attainment is attacked or sabotaged— usually by the power partner but at times by the passive-dependent partner.

A Decisive-Indecisive Relationship

These next two relational dynamics are interconnected and connected to the previous dynamics. The power partner appears decisive and sure of self; thoughts and opinions become inflexible. The passive partner can be indecisive and unsure of self. The passive partner goes along with whatever decision is reached by the rigid mate, despite silent disagreement with the decision. Many times the passive partner cooperates with the mate's leading without realizing that the passivity is itself assent to the decision or rule.

An Extremes-Oriented–Assenter Relationship

The power partner who is extremes-oriented sees the world in black and white. Everything is either all right or all wrong. Additionally, everything is usually the power partner's way or no way. Issues and circumstances are viewed as personal wins or losses. Any disagreement or resistance means that people may be considered the enemy, worthy of being attacked.

Because of the pleaser capacity, as well as the need to avoid conflict, the passive partner assents to the extremes-oriented worldview and perceptual experience of the power partner. The passive partner may try to convince the self of the power partner's correctness to dissolve feelings of uneasiness and discomfort. Psychologists call this *reaction formation*. The passive partner is psychologically capable of changing the mind toward a more comfortable point of view based more on relational pressure and unconscious needs rather than on the merit of the particular point. This support for the power partner's position reinforces the authority, decisiveness, power, and perceptual distortion. Too many times the passive partner yields to the demands of the extremes-oriented personality out of fear of rejection, retaliation, or abandonment.

It becomes easier and easier to see how a Jonestown experience, or a Waco Branch Davidian sect experience, can occur. The hidden danger is the deadlier, subtle ways such individuals can influence, frighten, alarm, and deceive the church community and the larger body of Christ, believing themselves to be righteous and being unswerved in their distorted perceptions of the truth for their perceptually misguided cause of Christ.

A Defensive-Conciliatory Relationship

The power partner can become defensive or jealous when power or codependency is jeopardized. This defensiveness often occurs in counseling situations. The power partner can be cooperative as long as the therapist is perceived to align with the power partner's opinions. If, however, the therapist is perceived as being aligned with the passive partner in any way, there is defensiveness or jealousy. The power partner will find some way to save the day: either by discrediting the therapist (e.g., "She's not Christian enough"; "She doesn't have the right credentials") or by applying intimidation or authoritarian tactics to convince the passive-dependent mate that continuing therapy is unnecessary (e.g., "Let's go see Pastor X or Counselor Y"; "All right, I've tried this counseling business, and I don't like it. Let's try to work this out ourselves with the Lord's help alone"; or nothing is said but the implication is, "Stop this or you'll be sorry!").

Of course, this reaction doesn't just happen with counselors. The same process can occur with family, friends, or church folks. The power partner is jealous of the person(s) who may sway the passive-dependent partner. The person(s) is seen as a threat, and tactics are begun to terminate any outside or hostile influence. The power partner who is severely jealous doesn't want the passive-dependent mate to develop support systems. The power partner resents the mate's being with others, especially on a regular and ongoing basis, and finds ways to keep the mate emotionally isolated.

This chapter examined some of the major possibilities by which a power personality and a passive-dependent personality may relate to each other. This chapter also developed the understanding of such a relationship as being codependent. Though not every relationship contains every one of these relational characteristics, none of these dynamics is healthy or helpful to a relationship. Each relational characteristic may represent a dysfunctional relationship or a dysfunctional family.

These processes are not necessarily deliberate, preconceived, or conscious. However, the self-destructive nature of the codependent relationship must be recognized. The destructiveness can be personal, relational, or corporal. This desolation can be deceptive and below the level of personal or relational aware-ness. It is also clearly both psychological and spiritual warfare. The next chapter discusses the concept of biblical submission in light of our understanding of codependency.

Chapter 6

SUBMISSION: FRIEND OR FOE?

Mary Givens was a submissive wife with a passive-dependent personality. Her husband, Hugh, had left one other time but had been home now for two years. Mary did everything she could to be a biblical wife. She tried to show submission, respect, tolerance, forbearance, forgiveness, and acceptance to Hugh, who had confessed to an affair during his departure. Mary knew she had biblical grounds for divorce, on the basis of adultery, but she wanted her marriage to survive.

Despite all her efforts, it seemed that Hugh continually lost respect for her and did things to deliberately test her. He requested that their marriage be an open marriage. Mary reluctantly agreed to it, though she had no intention of abandoning her marriage vows. She felt that she had no other alternative or Hugh might leave again. She knew that she needed to be submissive.

When Hugh kept staying out late at night only to return in the early morning hours or to return the following day, Mary certainly didn't feel very confident in herself or in her marriage. She learned not to lecture Hugh, and she remained relatively silent about her strong feelings of protest and resentment. She hinted at her feelings occasionally but was quick to back off if Hugh responded in an irate manner.

When Hugh drank too much and was loud, angry, out of control, and verbally insulting, Mary tried to make him feel better and tried to hide her hurt and upset feelings. Several times he grabbed Mary and was physically forceful. Hugh struck her on several occasions. Mary learned to live with the pain. What pain she felt on the outside was inconsequential to the pain that cried out from within her. She determined to turn the other cheek. She constantly forgave him and regularly prayed for him. She knew that she needed to be submissive.

It wasn't long before Hugh brought his dates home with him. His dates would sleep in the guest room. Hugh and Mary had long ago quit sleeping together. Hugh would tell Mary about each of his conquests and belittle Mary's previous sexual performance in comparison to present sexual partners. By then, Mary was significantly discouraged and depressed. She was increasingly numb emotionally to Hugh and to the mentally abusive way he treated her. She continued to pray for him and for their deteriorating relationship. But she tried not to upset or offend him. She tried to be gracious, self-controlled, merciful, and forgiving.

Mary pleaded with Hugh to go with her for marital counseling. He always laughingly refused. Mary sought individual counseling from her pastor, but she couldn't tell him the true picture of the depth of degradation of her marital situation. She was, however, able to present a demoralizing picture. Her pastor listened attentively and lovingly, encouraging her to be submissive to her husband. She wanted to know why her biblical behavior and submission had not won back her husband. She questioned why God would allow this to happen. She already knew that she needed to be submissive. She would continue to be submissive.

Biblical Submission Is Not Dishonor or Disrespect

Mary began to lose weight, and she experienced various physical problems. She fought terrible migraine headaches, which seemed to be increasing in regularity. She constantly felt tired, worn out, and discouraged. Mary even experienced a mild heart attack. She responded quickly to medical intervention and medication. Knowing the stress from her marriage was substantial, she continued to meet privately with her pastor. Her pastor had studied the principle of biblical submission, and he had considered its long-term effects. He discussed them with Mary. Both felt that it was clearly Mary's cross to bear. They further considered that God could be preparing her for some special ministry. And if the weight of her personal cross should become too unbearable, or if it should cost Mary's life, that, too, was considered worth it. After all, what did she have to lose by dying? She would go home to be with her Lord!

As extreme as Mary's situation appears, it is not rare in today's amoral world of cults and ambitions. Christians may be on guard to such worldly influences, but we are not immune to them. Some of these inducements are blatant, some are subtle, but all are deadly. We can be blindsided by various forms of these worldly influences, and we can be blinded by our psychological needs and coping resources.

God examines motivations.

In Mary's situation with Hugh, the picture of what is really going on is clouded by her sincere desire to be submissive in obedience to God's Word. Remember that God looks at our hearts (see Matt. 9:4). He examines the motivations behind the actions even when the actions appear biblical.

If Christ were to talk with Mary about Hugh, He would, no doubt, be pleased with her desire to be obedient to His Word as evidenced by her submissive spirit. He might, however, point out to her that submission was not her primary motivation. Rather, her primary motivation came from her emotional needs emanating from her passive-dependent personality. She needed Hugh.

If Mary's deepest thoughts and feelings (those that she could not immediately recognize) could be exposed, they would show that she was very frightened to be alone, fearful she could not make it without Hugh. She possessed all the characteristics of the passive partner. She was willing to tolerate his abusive and hostile behavior because it seemed safer to her than the alternative. She hoped that her biblical behavior, submission, and prayers would return Hugh to her. Though her response was based on the right biblical reasons, it was primarily based on the wrong psychological motivation. That is codependency. Mary was codependent rather than Christ-dependent.

The codependent partner reasons (usually at an unconscious level), "I'll do anything to get my emotional needs met. Show me what hoop to jump through and I'll do it. Just give me what I need." Sounds like a drug addict, doesn't it? Operationally, they are very similar. The Christ-dependent individual reasons, "I don't understand what's going on right now, but I trust Christ completely. He will meet all of my needs in His way and in His time. He's all I need. If He desires to give me back my mate, fine. If not, I'll learn to live without my mate for as long as it takes, even if this is permanent, by leaning entirely on Christ and trusting Him to work in my life to make me like Him through this difficulty."

Biblical Submission Does Not Allow Sin

In practice, Mary is also an accomplice in Hugh's sins and life-style. She is an enabler. Her behavior enables, allows, and reinforces his behavior. The behaviors and life-styles of both partners are products of sin, sinfulness, and/or their codependent relationship.

The apostles' statement in Acts 5:29 applies here: "We must obey God rather than men!" Though Mary's behavior appeared outwardly biblical, it was inwardly selfish. It was based on her needs and on Hugh's needs rather than on God's directive and the subsequent response of obedience.

God is a loving, caring, and gentle Father. He does not force Himself on us. We are capable of distancing ourselves from Him. If our mates enter into sin, it is not God's desire that we join them in disobedience. That is not biblical submission. We can remain prayerfully loyal, but we should not enter into sin with our mates. To do so would be to obey people rather than God and to go against the very fabric of Christian life and development. Certainly, Adam and Eve showed us this principle.

Due to codependent personalities, disobedience to God can be practiced in several ways. There is direct, defiant disobedience. There is disobedience by omission and commission of sin. There is disobedience by accident or mistake. There is disobedience by lack of discipline and lack of duty. And there is disobedience by vicarious action through the sanction of another's disobedience. Whether this sanction is realized or not is immaterial as far as a crime being committed. An accomplice to a disobedient act is still an accomplice and is also disobedient. That is not biblical submission.

Biblical submission means submission to God first and to one's mate second. Scriptural directives to submit to one's mate do not mean to disobey God. There are limits to submission to one's mate. If submission to one's mate contradicts submission to God, it is wrong. It is not of God. It must not occur. Sapphira was struck just as dead as Ananias while submitting to his authority and their deceptive plan rather than to God (see Acts 5).

So it is with codependent Christianity. Christian marriages can easily become codependent. This relationship is a perversion of biblical marriage. In Mary's case, submission is sinful. In most codependent relationships, submission is sinful. It is done for the wrong reason. It is done to satiate the flesh and to maintain codependency rather than to obediently follow Christ.

It can actually become idolatry. Does this mean that scriptural teachings, such as 1 Peter, concerning submission do not apply to everyone? Not at all. It even applies in power-passive relationships. Biblical submission is a central theme of Christian living. The heart attitude determines its righteousness. Biblical submission never contradicts God's Word.

First Peter is certainly correct in its teaching concerning submission. Chapter 3 wisely counsels wives to be submissive to their husbands, advising that the wife's very behavior has a tremendous witness and influence. Such biblical behaviors consist of chaste and respectful actions, deference, esteem, honor, appreciation, admiration, devotion, and love (the action if not the feeling—you do these things regardless of how you feel about doing them, but you implement godly limits to submission). Even when the wife is mistreated, her biblical goal is to work toward harmony, forbearance, perseverance, patience, love, and restoration.

In like manner, 1 Peter 3 addresses husbands to be understanding, considerate, honorable, respectful, and cognizant of the teaching that the wife should be considered the weaker partner. This passage is teaching not that women are inferior to men but that they should be treated as if they were weaker. Such recognition is like seeing them with a warranty card from the Creator, "Caution; handle with care; cherished, personal property of the Lord of lords." The husband also is instructed to work toward harmony, forbearance, perseverance, patience, respect, love, and restoration.

Chapter 4 stresses living for God and expecting suffering for being a Christian. When we are persecuted for righteousness' sake, we are to be glad and to rejoice in the participation of Christ's suffering. However, we can be persecuted for reasons other than righteousness. In a very real sense, codependency is a type of persecution. But it is not persecution for righteousness' sake.

Again, however, the matter of balance comes up. You have to admire Mary's decision to follow these teachings by loving

Hugh back into their relationship upon his return and even after his confession of adultery. At these points she certainly was depicting the love and submission that 1 Peter is talking about.

Separation and Divorce

If, in such a codependent relationship, submission can become disobedience to God or become idolatry, is there ever a point where divorce should be considered? Should Mary have left Hugh when his ungodly behavior continued?

Submission can be disobedience to God.

The Bible clearly teaches that marriage is a divinely ordained institution and is intended to be permanent (see Gen. 2:20–25; Mark 10:7–9). Nowhere in Scripture does God ever command divorce; however, He does permit it after the Fall because "your hearts were hard" (Matt. 19:8). There are two loopholes for biblical divorce: (1) sexual sin (see Matt. 5:32; 19:9) and (2) the departure of a nonbelieving spouse (see 1 Cor. 7:15–16). Neither loophole requires the ending of a marriage. God's desire is for restoration and healing. The book of Hosea shows us that God's love toward us is long-suffering, able to forgive such flagrant acts of betrayal and disrespect as adultery and departure. Though God's standards are high, He has provided loopholes because we are but dust and unable to match His standards. Yet His hope for us is that we will endeavor to persevere in our efforts toward His standards. He really doesn't want divorce at all, but He does allow it under certain circumstances.

This is not a book on biblical grounds for divorce. Though I believe there are certain, definite biblical grounds for divorce, I encourage you to remain in the marriage and to work hard at effecting healing and relational restoration. Only in the most serious of situations, and oniy after all of the suggestions presented in this book have been exhausted, should there be any consideration of divorce.

However, there may well be grounds for biblical separation. Even cases of biblical separation should be done with the goal of restoration. The important question for you to ask at this point is, What is God's will for me in a power-passive situation (that may be severe)? The direct, straightforward answer is to follow Him. Know and enjoy Him personally and relationally. Walk by faith and not by sight. Put Christ ahead of self and spouse. Ask the ongoing question, What would Christ do in my situation? And then do it. Know the limits of marital submission and enforce them. Stand tough for God, against self and spouse, when the situation threatens disobedience to God.

Beyond Biblical Boundaries

In Mary's situation with Hugh, she was being submissive to Hugh but disobedient to God. The Ten Commandments clearly cover adultery. It is plainly wrong. Yet Mary tolerated it wrongly in the name of submission. Mary seemed to show godly love in accepting Hugh back into her home after his affair. But she needed to critically examine her underlying motives. Mary later allowed adulterous and defiant behavior to continue in her very home in the name of submission. Her action (or lack thereof) was plainly wrong. It was based on her codependent needs. Her action (or lack thereof) enabled sin to continue.

Mary needed to set firm limits based on God's higher principle of submission to His Word. There were no consequences to Hugh's gross disobedience. There was no identification of sin or action to stop it. She was too tolerant of Hugh's behavior—in the name of submission.

God has the highest standards of love for us, yet there are limits to His tolerance (see Num. 14:18; Isa. 57:16) and consequences for our actions. He is not a kindly grandfather gushing out love to everyone, no matter what is going on. God can also be hurt and become angry. And there are consequences for disobeying God.

God has made many severe responses to disobedience. Scripture is replete with such instances. All the plagues struck Egypt because of Pharaoh's disobedience and God's reaction to him. Through Moses, God set limits, the limits were disobeyed, and the inevitable consequences followed (see Exod. 7—11). The Lord struck the Israelites with a plague for making a golden calf as an idol (see Exod. 32:34–35). The nation of Israel wandered around in the wilderness for forty years so that they could not personally enter the Promised Land. Moses himself was not allowed to lead them to the Promised Land because of his disobedience (see Num. 20:11–12; Deut. 3:21–28; 32:50–52). Aaron's sons, Nadab and Abihu, were consumed by fire for disobeying God (see Lev. 10:1–3). The list goes on and on. Numerous examples throughout Scripture demonstrate that God doesn't tolerate disobedience.

The principle remains that if we disobey God, there will be consequences for our rebellion. This happens in the New Testament as well. Ananias and Sapphira were struck dead for lying to God (see Acts 5:1–10). Jesus describes eternal punishment for those who demonstrate rebellion by not having accepted Him as Lord and Savior (see Matt. 24:30–35; Mark 9:43–48). Willful sinning is also the subject of divine consequence (see Rom. 6:1–2; Heb. 10:26–31). Jesus will rule over the ultimate dispensation of God's wrath (see Rev. 1:7–8, 17–18; 5:9; 22:12–19). Paul wrote, "Do not be deceived: God cannot be mocked. A man reaps what he sows" (Gal. 6:7). Though we can be misled, deceived, and deluded, God cannot be fooled.

God's Word is His love gift to us. It is not an army instruction manual. It is not restriction. Following God's Word allows us to grow and find spiritual fulfillment. It allows us to know and experience ultimate truth, freedom, and love.

Hugh and Mary's situation was a fairly straightforward one

and allowed us to consider the principle of hierarchical submission. That means we never submit to anyone or anything if it contradicts submitting to God's Word. In healthy Christian relationships, the first rule of operation and cooperation is to agree to always work at obedience to God's Word and to work together to ensure obedience is biblical.

Following God's Word is not always so clear. We have seen how submission can be unbiblical. To further complicate matters there are people with more than one personality flaw. There are power and passive-dependent personalities with additional confounding psychological problems. It can become a very complex problem to have rigidity or passive-dependency plus significant psychological and/or relational-familial dysfunction. The same principles apply, but it becomes much more difficult to ascertain exactly what's going on. What appears to be happening may not be happening, and what should not be happening may be wrongly happening anyway. The entire picture becomes increasingly muddled, distorted, and deceptive.

Dysfunctional Versus Dysbiblical

Dysfunction that leads to sinful behavior is always "dysbiblical." Gene and Sharon Yelton fit all of the criteria for a power-passive couple—and more. Both came from dysfunctional homes. Not only was Gene a power partner, but he experienced features of two personality disorders. Not only was Sharon a passive partner, but she experienced features of a personality disorder, an affective disorder, and a dissociative disorder. These diagnostic terms mean psychologically they were real messes.

Gene was a charmer. He was well-liked and respected in his church. No one suspected that he was very different at home. He was extremely controlling and demanding. He tried to control his wife through intimidation. It worked. She deeply feared him. So did the children. There was no physical abuse, but the mental and emotional abuse was cruel.

Gene was also extremely self-focused. Everything he did centered on meeting his needs. He was unable to care about or understand Sharon's feelings. He used and manipulated people to prove, to the Christian community, that he was a good Christian. He attended church regularly and sang in the choir.

He appeared saintly to the church leaders when Sharon left him. After all, she had an affair some years ago, and he had forgiven her, allowing her to stay in the marriage. No one knew that he had been involved in affairs, and he was presently committing adultery while trying to convince Sharon to return home.

Sharon appeared to be the bad guy since she left Gene. Gene used the information to sway church members to endorse his insistence that Sharon was the bad guy and must return home immediately. She had committed adultery years earlier. She regretted her affair and returned home to try to develop a healthy Christian marriage. Though she did not use Gene as an excuse, she later believed that he provoked her into an affair by his lack of love and by his emotional and sexual abuse. Sharon's feelings had all gone numb, and her affair was a desperate attempt to feel something—anything.

Sharon was discouraged, defeated, and depressed. Psychologically, she was a nonperson. She was like a robot who perfunctorily performed in a distant role as wife and mother. She was confused, detached, and frightened. She could not feel, and she tried not to think. She did not recognize her situation. She could not communicate her predicament. Though she screamed from deep within and hurt intensely, she could not express her need for help.

Sharon wanted very much to follow Christ. She believed her wifely role required submission to Gene's authority. She tried hard to be a submissive wife. Though she thought she was acting biblically, she felt cold, numb, resentful, afraid, and confused. She knew she was dying inside, and though she realized it was unbiblical, she perpetually considered suicide as a viable alternative to her present life-style. The only things that kept her alive and going were her two boys and her desire to follow Christ. Christ and her sons were her reasons to live and to try to awaken from her nightmarish existence. But when one boy attempted suicide and both boys disclosed their great pain, fear, and resentment toward Gene for emotional and sexual abuse, Sharon snapped out of her emotional fog long enough to determine to move out to safety. The realization precipitated a flight to psychological health. Gene was psychologically smothering them all, and they needed immediate relief. Sharon was able to comprehend the threat of the immediate crisis, and she took quick action to protect herself and the boys, though she still didn't fully understand it.

Gene demanded submission. Gene ordered Sharon to return home with the boys. He appealed to the church leaders who, without understanding the complete story, quietly and discreetly condemned Sharon's actions. Sharon didn't return. Gene remained in the choir, and he actively orchestrated church support for his position and against her actions. It appeared that Sharon was not submissive and not obedient to her husband, to her church, and to Scripture. But that was not so.

Sharon needed separation, even though she didn't understand biblical permission for it. She immediately entered into Christian counseling. She agreed that separation was only a temporary solution and a means of protection for herself and for her children. But it was also a means of protection for Gene. It prevented his sin of mental and sexual abuse, and it allowed time for Gene to deeply examine himself and to realign his life. In a very real sense, her brave action blew the whistle on the negative cycle of destructive behaviors occurring in their family. It was, therefore, a courageous, loving, and godly action. The codependent cycle was broken, at least temporarily. The abuse was stopped, at least temporarily. Sharon further agreed that her separation was a last resort option, and that she would actively work toward reconciliation. Gene reluctantly agreed and also entered into Christian counseling.

Power Leaders

A word of caution is necessary at this point. Just as there are power personalities, there are also power pastors, power church leaders, power authors, and power counselors. The power personality can assume a variety of roles. In seeking professional counseling, it is unwise to see a counselor who is rigid. There are well-meaning, albeit insufficiently trained, Christian counselors who would unhesitatingly admonish Sharon, who would have her confess her sin of rebellion and nonsubmission, and who would have her return immediately home to Gene. But it wouldn't work. It would only perpetuate the codependency. There is a lot of emotional, spiritual, and mental work to get done before reconciliation can successfully occur. There are well-meaning, albeit ill-equipped, Christian counselors who would not understand things like codependency, passive-dependency, detachment, depersonalization, and/or personality, affective, and dissociative disorders.

---

*Find a counselor who
shares your beliefs.*

What, then, are you to do? You should have an awareness of this possibility of getting a rigid or poorly trained counselor, but you should not be discouraged. Numerous qualified counselors are available, but you'll have to do some investigating to find them. Ideally, you want a counselor who shares the same beliefs and worldview as you do, and you want someone who has been trained and experienced in both psychology and theology. The more the shared values and beliefs, and the more training and experience the counselor possesses, the more likely you'll have a well-equipped counselor to help you in the healing process.

Check out the counselors in your area. Ask questions:

"What is this person's reputation in the community?"; "What training in psychology and theology does this individual possess?"; "What are this person's credentials?"; "What is this therapist like as a person?"

Sharon made a brave and tough decision in leaving Gene. But she was right. When she was with Gene, she remained so confused and chained to their respective dysfunctional roles that she was an enabler to ongoing sin. She was an accomplice by omission. Doing nothing reinforced the destructive cycle. By not protecting herself or her boys, she would be a participant in the actual sin.

Biblical Submission Is Hierarchical

Hierarchical submission was occurring. Even though Scripture teaches that wives are to be submissive to their husbands, it also teaches that husbands are to be submissive to their wives (see Eph. 5:21–28). Both are to be submissive to God. Being mutually submissive should not go against being personally submissive to God. Sharon was obeying God rather than a man. She was submissive to God but not submissive to Gene. Since Gene was blatantly engaging in ungodly behavior and was being rebellious toward God, Sharon was correct in not being submissive to him.

We Christians can be too quick to judge another's actions. Outwardly, Sharon could appear to be rebellious, and Gene could appear to be virtuous. We must not rush in to judge or to condemn.

Sharon's actions were biblically correct. She exercised tough love. She might placate the community of well-wishers and onlookers by returning to her passive partner role and appearing to submit. But it would only be an act. It would only perpetuate the deeper problems. The entire family would be sinning. There would be consequences for everyone's sins. There would be significant psychological damage. God would not be honored and could not heal and restore. Without repentance, there is no forgiveness of sins. To allow the destructive cycle to continue is to allow the renunciation of repentance and to allow the persistence of sin. It is disobedience and rebellion toward God. In such an instance, for someone to reject or condemn Sharon or her actions on the grounds of not being submissive to her husband, even if that someone was trying to be naively helpful, that someone would be participating in the destructive, sinful, and disobedient pattern.

Is submission a friend or foe? Submission is always a friend when it is biblical submission. Submission is always a foe when it goes against God's higher will, wisdom, and directive. Submission can be deceptive. Submission can fool the people about whom it involves, and it can fool the people about whom it revolves. It takes contemplative understanding and wisdom to expose the actual motivation and associative dynamic of submission.

As with the whole of Christianity, the concept of submission must contain balance. We are to be submissive to the right things and nonsubmissive to the wrong things. And the right and wrong things are not so easily detected—especially at face value.

The purpose of this chapter has been to broaden our understanding of obedience to God's Word and to create an awareness of various ways we can distort the truth. The next chapter focuses on defining the right kind of obedience and develops a working understanding of psychological and marital health that is honoring to God and conforming to His Word.

Chapter 7

THE SECRET TO A FANTASTIC MARRIAGE

I loved my dad greatly. He had a wonderfully warped sense of humor. Silly things tickled him. It didn't take much to make him laugh. No one else needed to laugh. Dad was going to enjoy the joke no matter what the social reaction. That nobody else laughed didn't faze him. If one other person did laugh, we were in for a long day. Dad would tell the joke over again or develop a new variation. I always loved it, even when I didn't think his joke for the fifth time was as funny as before. I quickly learned to look beyond the humorous situation itself and just enjoy my dad's enjoyment of life.

Dad had one joke that he must have told a million times. Each time, it was as if he had never heard it before. As soon as he would get started, I knew what was coming, and I would brace myself. Many times, he would tell me the same old recycled joke and break out laughing. He always did it. I always laughed.

The joke went something like this: ''Did you hear about the guy who went to the doctor?'' (At that point Dad would raise his arm up and delicately maneuver it in a protective fashion.) Dad would continue, ''This fella said, 'Doc, it hurts when I do that. What should I do?' The doctor replied, 'Well, then, don't do that!' ''

That's the joke. If you're waiting for the big finish, it's not coming. If you missed it, go back and reread the last paragraph.

What frightens me is that I must be getting more and more like Dad. This silly story still tickles me. Perhaps it's because it reminds me of him and happy moments. It occurs to me that maybe the joke reminded him of his dad, too!

Since becoming a psychologist, I've found that this joke is no joke. It's amazing how many times I've used this basic technique with a client. I always tell the story about my dad, too. I fear I really am becoming like him. Of course, the principle illustrated by the story is a bit more sophisticated, but it's the same result. It usually goes something like, ''Doc, she hurts me when I treat her like this.'' Then he identifies one or more infractions, such as his being insensitive, uncaring, thoughtless, disrespectful, demanding, controlling, and so on. The client then asks, ''What should I do?'' Guess what I say?

It's more complicated than that, but you get the general idea. This chapter is like that. It tells what *not* to do by showing what we *should* do. It presents a model for understanding Christian relationships as God intended them to be. It does that by looking theologically at humanity so that we can make sense of the model. The model helps us understand what we can do to have healthy, vibrant relationships that are psychologically and spiritually blessed by God. But it's not a quick and easy, one-two-three method. There is no such thing. It is a simple model that is complex at the same time. Understanding terms like *the Trinity* is simple yet conceptually complex. Since this model is based on the Trinity, it is simple yet complex, too.

There is nothing magical about the model, either. It will take a lot of hard work, determination, commitment, and persever-ance to make the model work. And the result must be a change in the way we live. But God will bless all attempts toward this kind of Christian living (even when we stumble).

Healthy relationships are hard work.

This chapter presents a general understanding of spiritual and psychological health for every Christian focusing on the power partner, the passive partner, and their relationship. The saying, "If you aim at nothing, you'll hit it every time," is true. A lot has been written about what we don't want in psychological development or relationships. Relatively little has been directed at psychological health, especially at functioning that is spiritually healthy as well.

Understanding Our Nature

We are going to consider an approach to understanding ourselves in relationship with God, in relationship with our inner selves, and in relationship with others. This trifold approach for understanding ourselves reflects the triune revelation of God as given to us in Scripture. Just as the Father, Son, and Holy Spirit are equally God, each dimension of a triune human being is equally valid. To quibble over which area is most important or which area should come second or third is to miss the mark. Like the Trinity, in which there are three separate and distinct persons yet one God, there are three separate and distinct dimensions of a human being, yet one human being. Created in God's image, a human being is functionally triune and holistic simultaneously. Like the triune Godhead, a human being functions as one in three and three in one: three different dimensions, yet one interfunctioning being.

Although Scripture speaks foundationally of a human being

as comprised of body and spirit or soul, it is useful operationally to consider a triune perspective. Although Scripture seems to support a view that at a person's constitutional level does not distinguish between soul and spirit, it seems to be that these distinct dimensions are different forms of the same substance. At the functional level, humankind interacts in a trifold manner consisting of body, psyche (or soul), and spirit. This discussion focuses on humankind at its psychological, functional level rather than its theological, constitutional level (essence).

I must interject that this view of humankind is not the ''only'' biblical view. Frankly, it is difficult, if not impossible, to adequately understand exactly how God made us! Such an understanding is too great for me personally and will remain one of the mysteries of God. I can appreciate different ways of understanding humankind, and I can tolerate other views consistent with Scripture and formulated with integrity, honesty, and spiritual conviction. I don't want my theological understanding of humankind at the foundational level to hinder another's understanding of the psychological applications deriving from it. It is beyond the scope of this book to present arguments discussing a human being, at the essence, as a dichotomy (body and spirit or soul) or as a trichotomy (body and spirit and soul). It is important that we don't get bogged down in theological arguments concerning the essence, or substance, of a human being as we focus on the functional, or applicational, level consisting of physical, psychological, and spiritual needs and operations. My understanding is that a human being is constitutionally dichotomous while functionally triune.

In examining a patient with brain injury, physicians would obtain CAT scans or MRIs (magnetic resonance imaging) to ascertain brain structure. Psychologists would implement neuropsychological assessment, with the same patient, to ascertain brain function. Both approaches are valid and complement each other. Similarly, the functional and applicational dynamic of a human being, which is represented by the triune model of this chapter, enhances and complements the constitutional understanding of a human being without detracting from it. The psychological model to be presented at the applied level is not necessarily restricted to one theological understanding of a human being at the presuppositional level. Functionally, a human being is spirit, mind, and body, and a human being is also spiritual, psychological, and relational. A human being is suprapersonal, intrapersonal, and interpersonal at the same time. An individual can have a personal relationship with Christ; a rich ability to think, analyze, and understand self (needs, wants, desires); and fellowship and relationship with others.

A Biblical View of Humankind

To accurately begin to comprehend humankind, we must incorporate this triune perspective. A human being is complex and wonderfully made, a physical, spiritual, and psychological being. Though a person functions as body, spirit, and soul, these separate dimensions can operate independently, or they can interact with one another. Sooner or later, however, each affects the other. For example, if I skipped a meal, my body would certainly be affected, but my psyche might not (at least not so readily or quickly). In fact, with my particular body, my psyche might react something like this: "Good job. You could stand to miss a few more meals! Keep it up. I didn't think you had it in you." If I missed several meals, my psyche might begin to react in a different way: "All right, you've proved your point. You can do it. Now how about some fuel for energy?" If I was deprived of food for long periods of time, my body, my psyche, and my spirit would begin to feel the effects. My psyche and my spirit would immediately team up for some sort of action. My spirit might say something like this: "I take these actions to mean we are spiritually fasting. Is that right?" And my psyche might reply, "I don't think he's spiritually fasting. He's making a deliberate attempt to lose weight, but he's going to extremes. I'm starting to feel drained and discouraged. I don't feel like doing anything. I'd like to find a couch and be analyzed.'' The body might chime in, ''Hey, fellas. Quit your bellyachin'. I'm shutting down the gastrointestinal tract and diverting blood flow to peripheral routes. Pray this doesn't go on too long. I like it best when we're all working together, and each of us is happy and contributing.'' ''Amen!'' declare mind, body, and spirit.

In the same way, a person can begin to neglect the spiritual life and not show any immediate impact on the psyche or the body, yet these areas will eventually be affected. I believe that the higher the quality of the spiritual life, the more readily will healing change affect the other two areas. There are a connection and a unity.

But to biblically understand humankind, we can't begin with humankind. We begin with God. Humankind will never be adequately understood apart from God. Humankind is properly defined and understood only in relationship with God.

A Biblical View of God

God is there. He exists and has existed eternally. He created us. He gave us an instruction manual that describes Himself, us, and our dilemma. The manual also contains the factory warranty and how to get the factory representative out to repair the damaged goods. But unless we have knowledge of God, we have only damaged merchandise with no understanding of its makeup, its purpose, or its operation. We can make guesses and try to make some sense of what is there, but we will always miss the mark if we do it without knowledge of God. We can know God only by God's revelation of Himself to us. God has graciously and miraculously revealed Himself to us in two ways: (1) general revelation (the world and universe about us), which should point us to God but does not reveal Him personally and relationally, and (2) special revelation, or His Word, the Bible, which discloses who God is, revealing Him personally and relationally, and further telling what this machinery we call life is really all about. It is the work of the Holy Spirit to illuminate the truth to us.

Appreciating the Pervasiveness of the Fall

We are relational and dependent beings who, having lost the original relationship with our Creator and the capabilities that relationship bestowed upon us, cannot bring about in ourselves those abilities necessary to function and relate in a fallen and sinful world. Such abilities come only from God. We need this primary relationship for true meaning and purpose, which are functions of a higher operative: they are ultimately a function of our relationship with God.

Meaning and purpose come from God.

Most of us don't fully grasp the pervasiveness of original sin and the Fall. We are still very much tainted. Even the things we think that we do have right are tainted. We need God and His truth more each new day.

When humankind fell in the Garden of Eden, the nature of human beings took a drastically different turn. The Fall resulted in a division between God and human beings, human beings and other human beings, and each human being and the self. Having been separated from God, we must be justified upon the basis of the substitutionary work of Jesus Christ. Though we are saved by grace, on the basis of Jesus' propitiatory work upon the cross, we yet bear the bruises, wounds, and scars of the Fall as we continue to grow as Christians.

A Biblical Model of Humankind

We can construct a model for understanding humankind based on the following propositions. First, human beings, created in the image of God, were specifically created for fellowship with God. Second, by virtue of Adam's rebellion against God, human beings allowed sin to enter into life, and all of humankind has become implicated due to the transmission of sin. Third, we can be restored to salvation by the proper knowledge of God by faith through Christ. Fourth, we find true and absolute meaning and purpose for ourselves by restoration of this relationship with God. Fifth, we still struggle and war against the flesh, and sanctification becomes a growth or developmental process whereby our commitment and submission to God and His will are cultivated by God. Sixth, our relationship with others becomes a function of our relationship with God. Seventh, our ability to grow in each of the trifold areas—knowledge of God, understanding of self, and relationship with others (or to deepen the level of understanding, commitment, and/or service)—directly affects our relationship in the other areas. Eighth, our growth in Christ (or the process of sanctification) is a continual process.

By way of illustration of this understanding of humankind, I will present two examples at different levels of the model. The first is the individual who has begun to understand self in relationship with God. The better the knowledge of God, the better the understanding of the need for Christ. As the person develops understanding of self, the better the person is able to relate to others the understanding gained for self. The individual develops a concern for others, which is shared as a function of the commitment to God. This function is not out of a sense of duty or command but flows directly from Christian freedom. Learning to relate in this way to others, the person gains new appreciation for God as well as a better knowledge of God, which flows the individual into another growth cycle. A growth cycle is a new round of spiritual growth that has sprung from the previous cycle. It means growth plus depth. My son's second season of basketball built upon the training, knowledge, and teamwork experiences of his first year. It could be considered that his first year represented one growth cycle and his second year represented another growth cycle.

Another example, but at a deeper growth cycle, would be the individual who, understanding self in relationship with God, implements gifts and abilities for building up the body of Christ. Using gifts to minister to the body, the person simultaneously understands self more fully while growing through active service to others. The relationship within the body gives the person better knowledge and understanding of God and God's will, which flow the individual into another growth cycle. The healthy individual is Christ-dependent. The person is growing triunely: in the knowledge of God, in the understanding of self, and in the relationship with others. (See fig. 7.1.)

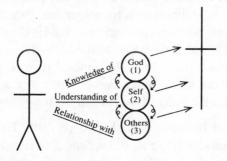

Level 1 is knowledge of God.
Level 2 is understanding of self as a function of level 1.
Level 3 is relationship with others as a function of levels 1 and 2.
Level 2 increases growth/appreciation of level 1. Level 3 increases growth/appreciation of levels 1 and 2.
A growth cycle represents growth from levels 1→2→3.
There is a cyclical effect in that the cycles are continual and rotational.

$$1→2→3→1→2→3→$$
$$→(cycle)→→(cycle)→$$
$$→→sanctification→→$$

FIG. 7.1. Christ-dependent growth model for understanding the dynamic of a triune human being.

Christ perfectly exemplifies the model. He lived a life of perfect submission to the will of the Father. He so completely denied Himself that, in submission to the Father's will, He laid down His life for others. Why did the Lord Jesus really come into the world? D. Martyn Lloyd-Jones offers this answer in *Studies in the Sermon on the Mount*:

> He came ultimately in order to deliver mankind from self. We see this selfless life so perfectly in Him. Look at His coming from the glory of heaven to the stable in Bethlehem. Why did He come? There is only one answer to that question. He did not consider Himself. That is the essence of the statement that Paul makes in Philippians ii. He was eternally the Son of God and was equal with God from eternity, but He did not consider that; He did not hold on to that and to His right to the manifestation of that glory. He humbled Himself and denied Himself. There would never have been the incarnation had it not been that the Son of God put self, as it were, aside.
>
> Then look at His selfless life here upon earth. He often said that the words He spake He did not speak of Himself, and the actions He performed He said "are not mine; they have been given to me of the Father." That is how I understand Paul's teaching of the self-humiliation of the cross. It means that, coming in the likeness of man, He deliberately made Himself dependent upon God; He did not consider Himself at all. He said, "I have come to do thy will, O God" and He was wholly dependent upon God for everything, for the words He spoke and for everything He did. The very Son of God humbled Himself to that extent. He did not live for Himself or by Himself in any measure. And the apostle's argument is, "Let this mind be in you, which was also in Christ Jesus."

Jesus came into the world so that the world might come to know God (see John 14:6; 17:3). If you don't know God personally, that's your first order of business. This book is directed to Christian couples, but one member (or both members), though using the name Christian, may not truly know Christ in a deep, personal manner. It is my prayer that this book will assist in pointing you to Him. If you do know Him, it is my prayer that this book will assist in pointing you to His will for you and your family in the midst of your present life situation.

J. I. Packer wrote in *Knowing God*,

What were we made for? To know God. What aim should we set for ourselves in life? To know God. What is the "eternal life" that Jesus gives? Knowledge of God. "This is life eternal, that they might know thee, the only true God, and Jesus Christ, whom thou hast sent" (John 17:3). What is the best thing in life, bringing more joy, delight, and contentment than anything else? Knowledge of God. "Thus saith the Lord, 'Let not the wise man glory in his wisdom, neither let the mighty man glory in his might, let not the rich man glory in his riches; but let him that glorieth glory in this, that he understandeth and knoweth me' " (Jer. 9:23f.). What, of all the states God ever sees man in, gives Him most pleasure? Knowledge of Himself. "I desire . . . the knowledge of God more than burnt offerings, says God" (Hosea 6:6).

We can know God only through Christ. We may know a lot *about* God without knowing Him. We must seek such knowledge of God through the person of Christ. That is why, on the figure of Christ-dependent growth, all three levels point toward Christ.

You can know God only through Christ.

From Jesus' example, we see that the self in the model is not a selfish one. We also remember that Jesus was not passive, either. He possessed godly self-esteem, and He lived a balanced life. The relationship in levels 1 (God) and 2 (self) is an intrapersonal one in that the individual is constantly working at conforming self in subjection to relationship with God. This primary relationship with God enables the individual to relate interpersonally at level 3 (others) on the basis of Christian freedom. The extent of the individual's ability to function intrapersonally with God and self directly affects the individual's ability to relate interpersonally with self and others. There is a cyclical effect in that the interpersonal relationship functioning with others enhances intrapersonal development of self through increased knowledge and experience of Christ.

The need for explanation of this last statement leads us to consideration of level 3 (relationship with others). It has pleased God to limit Himself in certain areas to the utilization of His people, particularly for building up the body of Christ by which the individual (a part of the body of Christ) attains toward mature faith and knowledge of the Son of God (see Eph. 4:11–16).

As expressed in 1 Corinthians 12, believers, or members of the body of Christ, are relational and dependent members of the body. This is the way it has pleased God to build up the body of Christ of which He is the Head. This is the way the believer has of discovering, implementing, and using those gifts and ministering abilities with which the believer has been endowed by the Lord. In so doing, the believer gains new insight, appreciation, and knowledge of the Lord, and how God has cared and provided for His own. In turn, this directly affects the individual's level 2 (self) development. This process allows development of self or biblical self-esteem. Nothing develops the self-concept like being used by Christ for His purposes through the work of the Holy Spirit by the gifts and abilities the particular individual possesses. The act of submissive ministry fosters Christ-dependency and feeds the Christian's self-concept. The self-concept is Christ-centered. There is a cyclical effect of each of the levels of development. The model stresses the holistic nature of a human being and represents a trifold breakdown of the process of sanctification.

The model demonstrates that the ideal relationship with one's mate must be considered from a triune perspective as well. Our relationship with others is a function of our relationship with God and our understanding of our inner selves. From a practical perspective, to earnestly desire a psychologically and spiritually healthy relationship with my mate and others, I must be willing to develop, pursue, and refine my relationship with God while understanding and developing my inner self as a consequence of this primary relationship. For any chance of spiritual depth and growth in my relationship with my mate, I must develop and maintain commitment and growth in my personal walk with Christ and let Christ grow and mature me from my innermost being. Simultaneously, I must be cooperatively willing and encouraging my mate to do the same. Figure 7.2 illustrates this principle.

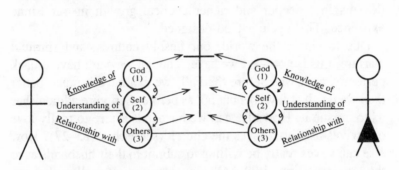

Level 1 is knowledge of God.
Level 2 is understanding of self as a function of level 1.
Level 3 is relationship with others as a function of levels 1 and 2.
Level 2 increases growth/appreciation of level 1. Level 3 increases growth/appreciation of levels 1 and 2.
A growth cycle represents growth from levels 1→2→3. There is a cyclical effect in that the cycles are continual and rotational.

$$1\rightarrow2\rightarrow3\rightarrow1\rightarrow2\rightarrow3$$
$$\rightarrow(cycle)\rightarrow\rightarrow(cycle)\rightarrow$$
$$\rightarrow\rightarrow sanctification\rightarrow\rightarrow$$

FIG. 7.2. Triune relationships.

The model depicted by figure 7.2 shows that relationships (level 3) are a function of knowledge of God (level 1) and understanding of self (level 2). Obviously, there can be some kind of relationship without the depth of levels 1 and 2 as a part of it. Yet such a relationship is limited and cannot flower into the relationship God desires for us as couples. He wants us to reflect Him. He wants us to enjoy the kind of love, harmony, fellowship, and joy that the triune God enjoys within Himself.

The model also reminds us that, as our triune relationship grows, we grow in our subsequent knowledge and understanding of God. In turn, we learn to understand ourselves more adequately, which in turn fosters deeper relationships, which flow us into deeper and richer cyclical growth in our triune existence. This cycle is God-designed.

Due to sin in the world, our fleshly natures, and spiritual warfare, this is not what we have. Though we can't have it back perfectly, as it was before the Fall, we can have it much better than we do. It still works but not as before. Scripture admonishes us to pursue it. How else can we husbands aspire to really love our wives as Christ loves the church (see Eph. 5:25–27)? How else can wives really be willing to submit to their husbands as to the Lord (see Eph. 5:22–24)? How else can we really submit to each other out of reverence for Christ (see Eph. 5:21)? How else can we really be imitators of God (see Eph. 5:1)?

Christ was our model. He was a leader who was a servant. He was obedient even at the cost of being nailed to the cross. He wasn't obedient for the sake of obedience. He was obedient as a function of His relationship with His Father and His commitment to Him. He was equal to God, yet was submissive to His Father. He wasn't submissive for the sake of being submissive. He was submissive for righteousness' sake. His self-concept was wholly predicated on His understanding of Himself in relationship with God the Father. He was a peacemaker but not at the cost of avoiding conflict. He loved the very people who hated and misunderstood Him. Yet He was not passive; He stood up for righteousness and stood against spiritual wrong. He was not rigid, either. He lived a balanced life.

Though He demanded righteousness and obedience to God, He knew the human heart and handled diverse people differently. For example, with the Pharisees, He could be pretty direct and outspoken. With His apostles, He used a variety of teaching approaches and interpersonal styles. He related to others on the basis of His knowledge of God and His understanding of Himself in this triune dynamic.

You are to be Christ-dependent.

Christ was love incarnate. His life showed all the fruits of such love. He was respectful, considerate, caring, confrontive, giving, humble, selfless, devoted, patient, gentle, kind, just, joyous, self-controlled, and God-centered. We are to imitate Him. We are to work at patterning ourselves after Him. We are to work at conducting our lives under the authority of His Word. We are to rely on the power of God to work this process in us. We are to reflect the triune dynamic of humankind. We are to work hard at Christian growth and development. We are to seek His face. All of these things constitute Christ-dependency. We are to be Christ-dependent.

Implications for the Power–Passive Relationship

Conformity to the Triune Model

The model has definite implications for Christian living within the power-passive relationship. As for all biblical relationships, the power-passive relationship must learn to conform itself to the triune model. Can it be done? Yes. The believer has the potential for overcoming sin—even the sin of a psychologically dysfunctional life. Will it be done? That depends on the individuals involved. Is it optional for the Christian life? No. Philippians 2:12–13 instructs us to

work out—cultivate, carry out to the goal and fully complete— your own salvation with reverence and awe and trembling [self-distrust, that is, with serious caution, tenderness of conscience, watchfulness against temptation; timidly shrinking from whatever might offend God and discredit the name of Christ]. [Not in your own strength] for it is God Who is all the while effectually at work in you—energizing and creating in you the power and desire—both to will and to work for His good pleasure and satisfaction and delight (AMPLIFIED).

Pursuit of God

Our responsibility is to pursue God, to pursue holiness, and to understand that Christ is cultivating holiness in us. The first and foremost implication is to go to God. We are to do this even if we don't feel like it or feel worthy of Him. We are to do this even if we are angry with our mates, upset with God, or hurting from emotional pain. It requires discipline in the most positive sense. And this requires continual, day-to-day seeking His face and yielding to Him. As we wholly pursue God, we cannot pursue other persons or objects that may influence us in a mutually harmful way. As such, we begin to provide change from our codependent, selfish, or sinful bent toward biblical Christ-dependency.

Responsibility for Self

Second, we are to take responsibility for ourselves. The most useless information is what "others" should do. We are to be teachable. We are to be willing to examine ourselves openly and honestly before God. We are *not* to blame. What we now feel is not a mate's fault, it's not a parent's or an employer's fault, and it's not God's fault (that we have chosen disobedience or that the effects of sin hurt us). We must be willing to see ourselves and our life situation as God sees us.

Being teachable means that we aspire to know God, His Word, and His will for our daily existence. It further means that we work at understanding ourselves and our relationships. This understanding must drive us to increased conformity to godly living. It means we look for resources and events to assist with this goal. If we need outside help, pride doesn't prevent us from seeking it. We perpetually work at this higher call to godliness while constantly monitoring our efforts to determine godly progress.

Responsibility for Relationships

Third, we are to take responsibility for our relationships. Successful relationships, which are psychologically and spiritually intimate, growing, and healthy, are functions of how well we do with our responsibility to know God and our responsibility to correctly understand ourselves in relationship with Christ. Practically speaking, that means if we want to learn how to really love our mates, we must learn how to know and love God in order to love our mates through Christ. Our love emanates from obedience to Christ rather than from feelings alone. And that also means if we want to learn how to love and accept our mates, we must learn how Christ loves and accepts us: "We love because he first loved us"(1 John 4:19).

A word of clarification is in order. This principle does not mean that to really love our mates, we pack up and go to a monastery. It does not mean that we throw ourselves into reading Christian books, going to Christian seminars, or attending Christian activities as events unto themselves. The book of James teaches us that there is a balance to Christian living: "But prove yourselves doers of the word, and not merely hearers who delude themselves" (James 1:22 NASB). The principle found throughout James is that merely knowing these things is insufficient. We must apply them. We must use them in a balanced way.

Practically speaking, that means we learn of God as we simultaneously give ourselves to our loved ones. Triune functioning and development are not either-or situations. It's a matter of doing both together.

The power partner who is extremes-oriented will find this triune dynamic difficult to understand. The extremes-oriented partner operates from a dualistic perspective—things are either one way or the other—not two (or three) things operating at the same time. Passive partners will need to push themselves not to be passive in implementing this triune model teaching. Christianity is not passive. Patience and long-suffering should not be confused with passivity.

Interdependency

The triune model also means that relationships are to be interdependent. One member is not independent while the other is dependent. Both cannot be dependent, and both cannot be independent. There is a triune balance to the interfunctioning of the relationship. Both members should be able to be independent but be willing to limit their individual strengths and abilities in a servantlike way. The couple allow themselves, from a position of strength, to become limited and dependent on each other for carrying out certain tasks, responsibilities, and functions that are helpful or beneficial to the life of the relationship. This is the nature of the concept of "one flesh." Both members seek to encourage and support each other's growth and development, and neither is threatened by the other's capabilities or performances.

Mutual Respect and Dignity

The philosopher Rodney Dangerfield correctly hit upon one of the real killers of relationships with his immortal words "I don't get no respect." Supreme levels of respect and dignity

---

Esteem, value, and prize your partner.

---

originated in the working of the Godhead. Christian relationships don't have a chance to survive and to grow without these core ingredients. Christian couples are to esteem, value, and prize each other and to actively communicate these things rather than assume the other person fully recognizes them. Our behavior toward each other is to be loving, honorable, and noble. Mutual worth and value are acknowledged and appreciated. We are to esteem the other person more highly than ourselves (see Phil. 2:3).

Tolerance Based on Christian Freedom

True understanding of our Christian freedom allows us to be open-minded and accepting of others (even when we don't accept the other person's behavior). Christian freedom means that, realizing our emancipation from the bondage of the law, we are freed out of love to seek obedience to God's will for us and to serve Christ because of our love for Him and our realization of our liberated commitment. We are to love the sinner and hate the sin. We are to be tolerant and patient without compromising Christian love or duty. Rigidity, control, and stubbornness are of the flesh. Christ has set us free from the power of sin, Satan, the law, and death. We are, therefore, appreciatively enabled to more fully love and serve our God and our fellow human beings.

Mutual Submission and Functional Equality

We are to be submissive to each other (see Eph. 5:21). Though the man is the designated spiritual head of the family, he recognizes this to be loving responsibility to God rather than a position of domination. He recognizes, utilizes, and appreciates his mate's functional equality, worth, and contributions. The woman accepts, respects, appreciates, and submits to the servant-leadership of the husband who loves her and follows Christ.

Christ-Dependent Self-Concept

Much has been written about the ego in psychological literature. The ego is the basic self. The self-concept must be anchored to the position in Christ. It is okay to feel good about loving and serving God. It must be remembered that God looks at our hearts (see Luke 16:15). It is too easy to feel bad about our Christian walk when we let others evaluate us for what they think we should be doing or when we incorrectly evaluate ourselves from our fleshly perspective. Ultimately, we are accountable only to God, and we will be answerable to Him. If, in whatever we do, our heart motivation is to obediently please God, we have reason to feel good about ourselves. But we must be on guard against wrongly pleasing God—thinking we are doing the right thing, feeling good about it, but doing the wrong thing. There are safeguards. Such actions will never contradict Scripture, nor will they cause harm or injury to the body of Christ. A helpful way of checking yourself is to establish some form of Christian accountability. Be willing to have godly people involved in a supportive way to help you evaluate yourself.

We cannot always go by the feeling that accompanies Christ-centered actions. The relationship of our feelings with our Christian self-concept has been greatly misinterpreted. We don't need to have good, pleasant feelings to obediently serve Christ. We can have positive feelings for many wrong reasons. And we can have negative or unpleasant feelings and obediently follow Christ. We are to go by the measure of our obedience and our heart attitude rather than by the associative feeling. At times in counseling sessions I have cried with clients. My feeling is obviously sad and unpleasant, yet my self-concept grows positively as I minister in Jesus' name. Feelings can fool us.

Communication and Time Together

We are to communicate well with each other, and we are to spend quality and quantity time with each other. Perfect harmony and communication exist within the Godhead. Because of our fallen world, however, we must push ourselves to communicate clearly. Doing all of the things listed in this chapter but not clearly communicating them to our loved ones and our God is like doing all of our homework but forgetting to take it to class. We don't get any credit. The giving part of our love and obedience is incomplete. We are to communicate our love and obedience.

That was epitomized for us by God when He communicated His love by sending His Son. He took great pain to be sure His message was received and understood. And His message continues to be beamed out twenty-four hours a day. God also communicated His love by showing us how to live and by providing written guidelines for us.

And Jesus didn't just show up and leave a message. He came in the flesh and lived among us for some thirty-three years. God gave us both quality time and quantity time. In today's hurry-up world, it's easy to sacrifice quantity for quality and feel it is acceptable. It is not. It is insufficient. It is not what God wants for us. It must be both.

The triune model represents something we are to work toward—an ideal for which to strive. Don't expect to attain it absolutely or perfectly. Anticipate that there will be times you just can't do it. But pick yourself back up and go after it. If you honestly seek to live this kind of Christianity, and you persevere with the right heart attitude with accompanying fruit, God is pleased and will bless you—even when you blow it. These things are the antidote to the disease of rigidity, passive-dependency, and power-passive relationships.

God is pleased when you try to change.

This chapter offers real hope for anyone desiring to break the bondage of the power-passive dynamic. Unfortunately, it is usually not so easily done in that one, or both, members may not be so motivated to pursue these things. The following chapters address the problem of not being able to change, either because of your fears or because of your mate's psychological blockade. There are tasks and strategies for overcoming these barriers. The affected individuals must change; the cycle must be broken; the dysfunction must be defeated.

Chapter 8

KEY ISSUES
FOR THE
POWER PARTNER

When I walk out of my office into the waiting room, I can get somewhat of an idea how things are going with my clients simply by observing their nonverbal communications. If a couple sit next to each other, smiling and holding hands, I remember the previous session, feel good, puff up a little, and anticipate another good session. That doesn't always happen, and my puff poops, but at least the session usually starts off well. On the other hand, if I observe the couple seated across the room from each other, I know it's going to be a long session.

I attended a meeting where nonverbal behavior was going on involving a power person. It was a large room with about twenty chairs assembled in a circle. On one side of the circle were ten people. On the other side sat the power person alone. I had to chuckle at myself upon noticing the arrangement since I had come into the room and had sat opposite the power partner before I realized what was occurring. Throughout the whole meeting, no one else seemed to make the connection. What was being communicated by the arrangement was that the person appeared to be oppositional and antagonistic to the others who had assembled in preparation for battle.

This chapter presents a picture of what the power partner is capable of doing to relationships. It's not a pretty picture. Obviously, not every power partner manifests every characteristic, but the power partner is capable of every single one of them. Some forms of rigidity are blatant and easily detected while others are subtle and may occur unnoticeably. Though the effects of any form of rigidity are felt by those on the receiving end, what has actually happened is not always so readily discernible—especially to the power partner. I hope that most power partners reading this book will be working to move from a more rigid perspective to a less rigid stance to no psychological or relational rigidity whatsoever. Again, the power partner is really not a bad guy and does not really want things to be going the way they are. Most of the time, such harmful and self-destructive results are not at all the preconceived strategies of the power partner. The power partner is usually not aware of the extent of what has happened.

Alienation Leading to Unrecognized Disrespect and Rejection

The power partner described in the above situation was oblivious to his impact on the people with whom he was associated. He had alienated himself from his peers without any idea of the effect he had on them. They expected noncooperation and resistance in some form, and the power partner usually obliged them. The alienation led to a loss of respect by the power partner's peers and subordinates. They joked about his rigidity when he wasn't present and rejected most, if not all, of what he had to say on the basis of his reputation as the power partner. He might as well have been wearing a scarlet *R* on his chest whenever he entered a room. The *R* stood at first for *rigid* and later for *rejected*.

As we have seen, there are degrees of rigidity, and there is an associated range of behavior for varying levels of rigidity. Even mild power partners (mildly rigid) are not fully aware of the impact of the rigidity. They oftentimes believe all is well and they are doing a fair job commandeering their crew. Others won't usually sound the alarms even when the ship has huge gaping holes in its stern. Too many times, power partners discover the effects of the holes only when there's not too much left to do about them. They have injured others, usually unknowingly, and the wounded persons have begun to protect themselves. Power partners can't grasp why others seem to have turned on them for no apparent reason.

Severe power partners (severely rigid) encounter many situations like the one above. Mid-range power partners (moderately rigid) encounter it in a lesser version, often wondering why people seem to be contentious, oppositional, or uncooperative. Mild power partners encounter resistance but are able to back off, recognizing that they may be coming on too strong or may be appearing tyrannical. Any rigidity produces a natural strain and subsequent interpersonal distance in relationships.

If power partners (mid-range or severe) have any sense of awareness at all, they detect that something is wrong and withdraw. They are seldom fully aware of what has happened and end up blaming someone, or the group, for being unfair, non-Christian, hypocritical, dictatorial, and so on, thus justifying their ensuing departure. They can't get along with others in a mutually cooperative fashion, nor can they control others. This inability usually causes frustration and eventual renunciation of whatever, or whomever, seems to be resisting the demands of power partners.

Focusing Objectives

This chapter presents an overview of specific objectives that are important for the power partner to overcome to be successful in relationships. Not all objectives apply to every power partner; however, the more rigidity the individual possesses, the more objectives there will be to overcome. The mild power partner will have fewer applicable objectives than will the severe power partner. Even the mild power partner needs to be aware of the natural bent toward more dysfunctional behavior if left unchecked. Awareness of any possible difficulty allows early detection and a better prognosis.

The power partner (rigid personality and/or rigid marital role) must learn to overcome

- lack of awareness of rigidity and become aware of how rigidity affects and destroys relationships.
- lack of openness; defensiveness; and unteachability.
- the appearance of opposition; antagonistic views; alienation; and the appearance of lack of cooperation.
- an intense need for control in relationships.
- lack of conformity to the triune model; lack of Christlike servant-leadership; and lack of development of servant-leadership for the mate and family.
- lack of self-denial; the inability to love the mate unconditionally; or the inability to love without jealousy or insistency.
- lack of taking ownership or personal responsibility in problem areas; blaming others for problems.
- intimidating behaviors designed to maintain control while discouraging growth and autonomy by the mate (intimidating behaviors include, but are not limited to, criticism, ridicule, and manipulation, e.g., guilt trips, threats).
- lack of intimacy; interpersonal insensitivity; poor communication; and sexual selfishness.
- insecurity; self-doubt; and codependency.
- resentment of authority; intolerance of different views; "my way or no way" attitude; and close-mindedness.
- pride; the inability to admit faults or weaknesses; the inability to ask for help or to receive help when offered; and lack of accountability.

Winning a Losing Battle

The power partner may be willing to change for a very good and basic reason. The power partner is fighting a losing battle. The power partner holds many wrong assumptions but is not fully aware of them. Steadfastness, discipline, and perseverance are confused with justification of a rigid life-style. The power partner needs to have control in relationships, yet stands to lose not only control but the relationships themselves! Time is running out, and things won't start looking better. Even in relationships where there is only mild rigidity, marital dissatisfaction is likely, and change is also mandated.

Submit to your passive mate.

A great paradox is involved. There is a way for the power partner to obtain relational control and keep it. This kind of control involves becoming a biblical shepherd, or servant-leader, of the home. It involves pursuing the triune model of living. It involves loving the mate the way Christ loved the church. It necessitates gaining control by giving it up. The purpose of this chapter is to further clarify how to do that. There is strength in weakness, victory in surrender. This paradox constitutes the essence of Christian freedom. The books of Ephesians and 1 Peter speak directly to leadership in the marital relationship. It is no coincidence that both books address the notion of biblical submission as preliminary and foundational to servant-leadership. There is success in submission, triumph in obedient acquiescence.

Developing Self-Awareness of Rigidity

One of the first goals of power partners is developing awareness of this sense of estrangement and alienation by the rigid way of life. It means facing the possibility that they may indeed be rigid and not recognize the rigidity or the extent of the rigidity. It also means facing the probability that others don't want to be around rigid people for any length of time unless they absolutely have to. Even then, it is tolerated rather than appreciated. Mild power partners are open to these possibilities and earnestly want to defeat them to grow personally, relationally, and spiritually. They may wonder why long-term, close relationships (especially outside marriage) seem to become problematic or to go sour. Mid-range power partners resent the notion that they may be rigid or more rigid than they are willing to admit. They will reluctantly deal with the realities of the rigidity if they are firmly and lovingly encouraged to do so. More likely, they find that they have to do so because their lives have begun crumbling due to the naturally destructive effects of rigidity. Severe power partners will have nothing to do with such psychological nonsense! They will resist awareness for themselves and for their mates and fight it every step of the way.

This resistance to the truth is due to the age-old problem of pride. Power partners are proud. They find it difficult to ask for help. But like everyone else, they must learn to push themselves to honest self-examination, which leads to personal growth, especially now that the cover is blown. Passive partners now know power partners' core reasons for being rigid are directly related to their feelings of insecurity, their fear of lack of control (which leads to rejection and/or failure), and their subsequent pride that hinders them from personal growth necessary to maintain relationships. On the other hand, if people sincerely study the information covered in this book and apply it to themselves (without blaming, or dragging in, others) with the objective of improving themselves and their relationships, such actions warrant genuine hope. The healing process has begun.

Conforming to the Triune Model

The most important goal of power partners is the ongoing task of conforming to the triune model. If power partners are willing to pursue personal development in adherence to the principles of the triune model, there will be positive growth, victory, healing, and blessing from God. Just going through the motions alone won't do it. If the heart motivation is pure and earnest, God will surely reward the efforts. This conformity is the paradox mentioned previously. By surrendering control to Christ and living out the triune model, former power partners make possible the submission of their mates in the biblical manner. The demonstrated recognition of submission to Christ and the desire to love the partner as Christ loves the church make it possible for the former power partner's mate to be won back over time.

Denying Self

Denying self means putting on Christ and living out the triune model. This is hard for all of us but especially for the power partners. Of course, the more rigid the people, the harder self-denial becomes. If people are really not born again, or if they are not fully committed to Christ, it will show up here. On the other hand, if there is a bona fide conversion experience, there is real hope—even for severe power partners. This hope, however, doesn't mean that people will automatically change, but they can change with Christ's help. I have witnessed severe power partners overcome their rigidity by spiritually choosing to really lean on Christ, by psychologically choosing to work through any barriers frustrating this Christ-dependence, and by volitionally choosing to actively pursue the triune model. There is hope for even die-hard power partners.

Severe power partners may be Christian more in name than in deed. Though they may do many of the right things, it may be for the wrong reason, or it may accomplish wrong results that may be more destructive than helpful. They likely won't see the destructive part because the harm is to others and not to them. They may not be open to scrutinizing their motivation, and they may be insensitive to the damage (or extent thereof) done to others.

Mid-range power partners will face some of these same obstacles, though to a lesser extent. Their damage may be less, but their rationalizations will be greater. They may be able to notice the harm but try to minimize, ignore, or defend their actions. They may try to bend Scripture to suit their views or find other confirmation of their particular bias, view, or need. This may include discrediting other Christians or authorities who don't view the world or situation as they do. Such admonition may come in the form of criticism, blaming, or faultfinding.

Mild power partners will most likely be concerned about the possible destructiveness of the rigidity, especially on loved ones. They are quite capable of converting unhealthy, rigid features into their healthy counterparts of old-fashioned discipline and perseverance. They are able to use information to effect biblical change. They respond well to encouragement, structure, and praise. They desire to follow Christ and to pursue the triune model of Christian living. They are able to sacrifice needs to accomplish this.

The Need for Confession, Repentance, and Forgiveness

Along with awareness comes the responsibility for confession, repentance, and forgiveness. If there is any recognized rigidity, the individual has, at a minimum, automatically wronged God, spouse, and self. The primary sin has been against God, but the secondary sins have also been harmful.

*Forgiveness, like change,
is a process.*

Upon recognition of rigidity in any of its various forms, the power partner's duty, out of love, is to confess the rigidity to God, to commit self to genuine change with repentance, and to ask God for forgiveness (see 1 John 1:9). The next step is to do the same thing with the mate. These same actions may be appropriate with others (e.g., children, family members, friends, etc.). Once such actions are initiated, relational healing begins to occur.

Forgiveness is a process in power-passive relationships. It is not a quick fix, and the offended party's injured feelings do not just disappear. The power partner must understand that all forms of rigidity do not automatically stop. Though the power partner may try to overcome significant parts of rigidity, some forms are going to continue to occur. Termination of rigidity is a slow and painful death. Trying to turn the tables on the passive partner for being unable to completely forgive is very unfair and evidence itself of continuing rigidity. A more realistic and workable approach is based on the recognitions that (1) forgiveness is in order, but it must be based on real repentance or change from previous behavior; (2) change from a rigid lifestyle is a process, hence forgiveness is a process; (3) the injured party can forgive previous offenses, yet still be sensitive and reactive to different forms of continuing rigidity; and (4) power-passive forgiveness requires patience, perseverance, and a working understanding that the relationship is in the process of being repaired.

An agreement such as the following might clarify this forgiveness process:

To My Dearest Beloved:

I now know that I have hurt you with my rigid life-style and behaviors (*list as many as you can*). I truly am sorry, and I ask your forgiveness. I am learning how to become more Christlike and less rigid. As I grow in my personal and spiritual development, I pray I won't injure you anymore. Yet I fear that, since these patterns are so ingrained, I might unknowingly harm you. This is not what I want. Please point out any ongoing ways my rigidity may be occurring. I want to stop them all, and I need your help to do so. I love you very much, and I am committed to becoming the kind of spouse that Christ wants me to be for you.

Loving the Mate As Christ Loved the Church

For the passive partner, self-denial tends to be weighted too much on the side of complete loss of self; for the power partner, self-denial tends to be a lost art altogether. The passive partner errs in neglecting self in the wrong way. Such self-denial is not biblical or balanced. The power partner errs in focusing too much on self and may even view compromise as losing. Such lack of self-denial is more obviously unbiblical. Pursuit of the triune model necessitates balanced Christianity.

It takes time, and there are many slips and a few blunders along the way of developing the triune mind-set and response to Christ. Christ-dependent individuals realize that they won't be able to do a perfect job, but they pursue the triune model. Christ was our example. He denied Himself to the ultimate extent at the cross.

Denying self also means that power partners put their mates ahead of themselves. They become more concerned with their mates' needs, feelings, and welfare than with their own. They work at learning what it means to "love their wives, just as Christ loved the church" (Eph. 5:25–33), and then they work at implementing that kind of love.

They recognize that the natural tendency is to do the opposite: to unconsciously concentrate on themselves to the neglect of others. They understand the victory that is theirs in Christ despite the battle of the flesh and the old nature (see Rom. 6:1—8:17). They triumph over the naturally destructive needs of rigidity and codependency. They become servants (see Matt. 20:26–27; 23:11–12; 25:23). They develop a mind-set that puts others ahead of themselves. They seek to develop empathy and compassion toward their mates. They encourage and promote their mates' Christ-dependency. It pleases them to observe, and to participate in, their mates' growth and development spiritually, emotionally, and psychologically. They are not jealous but secure in servant-leadership. They model a balanced approach to relationships. Their ability to love, and to be loved, ascends to new heights.

The Confrontation of the Two Kings

One of my first internships at a psychiatric hospital did wonders for my naivete. I was assigned to watch a new patient and to intervene should there be any destructive behavior. I watched him practice meditation for about fifteen minutes. He seemed calm and well in control of himself.

As we were leaving the area, he pointed to a blackboard and asked me what I thought of the poetic writing on the board authored by a person who called himself Merlin. I tried reading it only to discover it was entirely gibberish. The patient confided to me that he was Merlin. He also let me know of his more appropriate title of King of the Universe. I was a bit taken aback, but I quickly remembered where I was.

Two days later I admitted a new patient to the unit. Among other interesting bits of information, I learned from the new patient that he was King of the Universe. How about that? Two kings of the universe right there on the very same unit! Had their situations not been so tragic, I probably would have seen the humor in the situation then. Instead, I began to be concerned about a meeting between the two kings and the psychological impact of such an occurrence—especially if they discovered each was King of the Universe. You just can't have two kings of the universe, and each would know that.

It happened the very next day in a back hallway. I ached that I missed it. I saw the second patient later that day and inquired if he had yet met Merlin. He told me of their meeting. It was short and dignified. The two kings met and got right down to business. I asked him specifically if anything significant happened, wondering if the feared topic came up. He advised me in a matter-of-fact manner that their conversation had gone well and that he was now officially Assistant King of the Universe.

Controlling the Controller

The way it went for the two kings is strikingly similar to the way it goes for the two members of the power-passive dyad. It's not usually so contestable, and many times is much more subtle, but the same kind of power struggle occurs. Many times, in other relationships (e.g., work, church, etc.) the power partner encounters resistance with trying to run things. This is especially true if the other relationship involves another power partner. Then a situation like that of the two kings clearly arises. Unfortunately, there is no assistant king when severe power partners are involved. In situations where the severe power partner comes in second, the person almost always leaves the situation ("I'll take my ball and go home"). After all, the power partner can go somewhere else to reign: home to the passive partner.

Power partners have a deep need to feel in control. This need comes from a deeper insecurity. The deeper the insecurity, the greater the need to feel in control. Severe power partners would not be aware of such needs and would fight anyone, tooth and toenail, who might suggest such a thing. They often employ intimidation against anyone who might start questioning, or uncovering, their ways and motives. Such threats may not work with everyone. When they don't, the next means of self-defense is to retreat. This departure is a type of avoidance and is often accompanied by some "legitimate" reason to justify, and cover up, their escape.

Maintain good, supportive dialogue.

A deep fear of severe power partners is that if their mates learn to function on their own, they might not need the power partners or tolerate the rigid characteristics. Hence, they frustrate their mates' efforts at growth and Christ-dependency because they need to continue the codependency.

Power partners must show acceptance of the game plan of change from codependency to triune functioning. They should demonstrate leadership toward this new goal without giving the perception that they are being domineering. This transitional work can become confusing: "I demand that we quit being demanding!" Keeping good, supportive dialogue going, while instituting new behaviors, goes a long way in overcoming the appearance of domination.

Creating and Nurturing Servant-Leadership

Another goal for the power partner is relinquishing the controller role while continuing in the servant-leader role of the triune model. Encouraging the mate and the family to learn servant-leadership is a task the shepherd of the home models, teaches, and cultivates.

My family loves to go to Disney World. When the Disney/MGM theme park opened, we felt obliged, as old friends of Mickey's, to investigate the new part of the Disney theme parks. Naturally, we revisited all our old favorite parts, too. It worked out particularly well because there were three parks and we had three kids, each of whom had unique ideas about what to do.

At that time, Peter was ten, Carrie was eight, and Christine was four. My wife, Linda, and I came up with what we thought would be a pretty good idea targeted at this notion of cultivating the concept and experience of being a servant-leader.

Christine had the leadership role for the entire family at the "Magic Kingdom," Carrie had the leadership role at the MGM park, and Peter had the leadership role at Epcot Center. We attended each on a separate day. Each child was responsible for every decision made that day—from where to go to what to eat. The children were keenly aware that, though they were in charge at a particular time, they would not be in charge when they weren't the assigned leader. Each child knew the basic principle of "doing unto others as you would have them do unto you." More practically, they understood "if I am nice to my brother or sister, he or she will be nice to me." It was amazing how considerate each leader was of what the other two wanted. It was just as amazing to watch how the two, who were not in charge, cooperated and submitted to the servant-leader's care.

Since Christine couldn't read, I was unsure how well she would respond to the situation. As I was bending down to take her on my knee and give her some fatherly comfort and assurance, she took off toward the Dumbo ride, giving instructions to the other two along the way, like a general planning to invade enemy territory. She told Peter and Carrie of her wishes while obtaining feedback from them about what they wanted to do, too! I was stranded in my paternal position while she shot off confidently as if she had been doing that sort of thing for years. All three children responded favorably to the opportunity to assume leadership. Each was sensitive to the effects of leadership. This family event allowed a positive exercise, which helped each child learn the basic idea of servant-leadership and be successful at it.

Double Duty

The power partner often wears two hats: family shepherd and spiritual head. At the very least, the power partner is the shepherd for the children and is instructed to be submissive to the mate. If the power partner is a husband or a dad, he automatically is the family shepherd. As the head of the home, the power partner is to put personal needs aside in order to advance the spiritual and psychological maturation of the family. He is to actively look for ways to accomplish this while creating an awareness of his own blocks in this process and subduing and eventually overcoming anything that gets in the way of presenting them faultless and holy to Christ (see Eph. 5:25–27).

The family shepherd ensures that his wife knows how to do things without him (e.g., manage the checkbook, establish social and spiritual relationships and disciplines, develop career objectives, etc.) while he continues to be available to her throughout her preparatory process. He is also ready and willing to do the work for her should his help not impede or hinder her capabilities, or should she already possess demonstrated proficiency in the area but choose not to exercise her expertise. Once she has learned to change a flat tire by herself, it is no longer necessary for her to change all flat tires!

The Fizz of the Wiz

Power partners must go against the grain of their personalities when their naturally destructive tendencies begin to surface. However, saying it should be done is much different from actually doing it. Severe power partners will find this transfer of power to be extremely uncomfortable. They will fight it at one level even when they want to yield control on another level. One way they will fight it is by intimidation.

Remember the movie *The Wizard of Oz*? Toto discovered that the imposing image of the wizard was a facade designed to elicit fear and submission. The wizard was just another human who resorted to trickery to maintain the illusion of control. It worked well until Toto tipped off Dorothy, who unveiled the bewildered wizard and exposed his fraud. By now, you are probably well ahead of me. The power partner is like the wizard, trying to intimidate others, particularly the passive-dependent mate, by creating deceptions that allow the continuance of the conscious and unconscious agenda.

The intimidation varies according to the level of rigidity. Severe power partners may employ fear, threat of harm, or actual physical and/or psychological abuse. Mid-range power partners may employ criticism, ridicule, deprivation, social or occupational isolation, and/or discouragement. Like severe power partners, they try to undermine their mates' self-confidence or to sabotage attempts at independence. Mild power partners may exercise too much "love" for their mates so that the mates' abilities are overshadowed by caretaking behaviors. Mild power partners, though, are different from mid-range and severe power partners. They really do want what is best for their mates but are often blind to their own negative impact. With just a little awareness, they are quick to recognize errors and to correct them. Mid-range power partners are harder to reach and slower to change. Severe power partners will fight the notion of intimidation, defend their actions, and continue with the same behavior patterns (hoping the entire matter will be dropped or forgotten). They become upset if their passive-dependent mates won't allow the matter to drop.

Power partners are good bluffers who seldom have their hands called. Passive partners often do not realize that power partners are not so formidable as they appear. Mild power partners and mid-range power partners are capable of responding to loving confrontation about these matters of control and intimidation. Severe power partners must be handled with caution. Their reactions can vary. They will almost always react negatively to such a confrontation. They may respond favorably and be reluctantly forced to change by loving but firm mates who see behind the veil. But they may respond unfavorably and become verbally, emotionally, and/or physically explosive or violent. If such a response seems at all likely, good Christian counseling and protection become musts. Skilled helpers can maneuver couples through the winds of control and the squalls of intimidation.

Control is unbiblical.

The goal for the power partner is to give up intimidation and control altogether. Control, based on the needs of the power partner, is unbiblical and won't work. In the short term, it may seem to be effective, but it will eventually self-destruct. Again, the power partner may win the battle but will surely lose the war. The major point here is that control and intimidation will not work, hence the rigid approach is inevitably bound to fail. The power partner will eventually lose complete control and may already be aware of the dwindling ability to maintain it. How hard the power-passive family falls depends upon how long it takes the members to realize their collective and individual plights and upon how long it takes the members to individually and collectively change course. Even in cases where the power partner is severe, there is still genuine hope if that person is willing to allow Christ to effect changes from within.

The Martyr's Routine

One of my friends told me about his mother. He disliked the way she manipulated him. If he didn't do pretty much what she wanted, she went into the captivatingly lyrical martyr's lament: "How can you treat me this way after all I've done for you? You should be ashamed of yourself!" That was the main refrain, but there were hundreds of verses—all of which cited how much the poor mother had done for her little boy who didn't appreciate her and who owed her recompense. Maybe you've heard the song. It's certainly not unique to my friend's mother.

Power partners may also pursue this course of action. They use it as a power tactic and a way to maintain control: "After all I've done for you, you owe me. I'm so good to you. How can you treat me this way (wanting to take away my control)? You should be ashamed of yourself!"

Power partners must be sure they don't perform the martyred mother routine. They must be careful not to employ threats or guilt trips as manipulative tools. Incidentally, it doesn't work for mothers, either. It may produce an effect, but it's not the effect anyone really wants, especially in the long run.

The Violation of Intimacy

Power partners are usually unaware of their interpersonal insensitivity and thoughtlessness. They believe they are sensitive, but they are not adequately sensitive in an others-oriented manner. Mild power partners assume they are sensitive if they remember to take out the trash that day. Mid-range power partners feel they are adequately caring if they don't complain about the seasoning of the meal. Severe power partners believe they are doing well not to yell or get physical when food or drink isn't hot or cold enough.

These admonishments pertaining to relational intimacy especially apply to the sexual area. Power partners need to focus on their mates' needs. Such needs include not only obvious physical ones but also emotional and personal needs.

Too many passive-dependent women endure masculine-oriented sex while sacrificing their sexual fulfillment. And severe power partners don't usually notice! I recall one frustrated passive-dependent wife who, afraid to express her dissatisfaction to her rigid mate, tolerated sex his way by visualizing another man while making love. She knew it was wrong, but she couldn't face the probable conflict that refusing sex or honestly confronting would ignite. She was in a no-win situation. Clearly, it was the power partner's fault for allowing such a situation. It was equally the passive partner's fault. Whether it was a sin of omission or commission by the power or passive partner really didn't matter.

I realize that I'm overstating my case, and I apologize if I sound sarcastic. But for the passive partner, sex without intimacy, especially on an ongoing basis, can begin to feel like emotional rape. And without intimacy, there is no substance to any relationship. The woman fantasized a previous lover who treated her tenderly and kindly when she made love with her rigid husband who, focusing on his needs, neglected emotional intimacy. She only did it because she knew of no other way to be submissive while enduring feelings of emotional and relational violation.

Mid-range and severe power partners aren't tuned in to their mates' needs. Communication is dictation. Consideration is self-gratification. *Tenderness* and *thoughtfulness* are merely words in old songs sung by Elvis.

The rigid male has not fully developed the idea that his mate may be different from him. He has not fully recognized or respected his mate's femininity or personhood. He has difficulty understanding or honoring differentness. She mechanically performs for him and carries out her duties responsibly. There is no place for biblical love in a robowife. God didn't make us robots. We have the freedom to love Him or to reject Him. When we do love Him, it is not automated and programmed but free, deep, personal, unique, complete, and responsive. Similarly, when we give our mates freedom of personhood and freedom to love, they can respond with new dimensions of true, biblical love.

Power partners must learn to develop intimacy. They must work at developing availability, openness, empathy, tenderness, compassion, thoughtfulness, and communication. They must be willing to learn how to please their mates. They must be willing to learn how to prize, respect, and esteem their mates above themselves.

The Power-Passive Relationship Is Abusive

The power-passive relationship is characterized by varying degrees of abuse. The range of abuse can vary from disrespect to psychologically destructive games to emotional (and some-times physical or sexual) abuse. Obviously, there is no place for any abuse in any healthy relationship.

Severe power-passive relationships contain obvious abuse. Mild power-passive relationships contain minimal abuse and marginal felt-harm. By felt-harm, I mean damage that is recognized and realized. Though power partners may not recognize their abusive impact, they should look for signs of the felt-harm in their mates. Such signs include, but are not limited to, anger, depression, fear, complaining, criticism, anxiety, panic attacks, resentment, withdrawal, avoidance, sleep problems, nonspecific physical complaints, tension headaches, and/or lethargy.

Look for felt-harm in your mate.

Some characteristics of abusers are similar to previously discussed characteristics of power partners:

• Poor communication skills. Abusers cannot appropriately express feelings.

- Poor self-image. Abusers don't feel very good about themselves, and they feel unable to control their world. Subsequently, they try to compensate by a false sense of control via intimidation or violence.
- Inability to understand deeper personal feelings of anger and frustration. This anger is displaced onto the spouse.
- Jealousy of spouse. Therefore, there is a need to control the spouse.
- Feelings of dissatisfaction, frustration, or oppression.
- Appearance of sociability. Abusers may not have any other abusive relationships and can appear socially competent.
- Abusive experiences from the past. They may have been abused, in some form, as children. Consequently, abusers learn abuse as a part of a sense of family normalcy.
- Experience with alcohol or other drugs, which disinhibits restraint.

Admitting Insecurity

The power partner is reluctant to admit faults or weaknesses. No one wants to be identified as an abuser, yet the power partner, by very nature, is abusive. It is hard for the power partner to recognize flaws, to ask for help, or to receive help when it is available. Like the apostle Peter, the power partner would balk at the Lord's washing of the feet.

One of the power partner's primary secret tasks is to hide self-doubts and insecurity. The power partner tries to ensure that no one discovers the abusive styles of relating, but others will eventually feel them even if they don't clearly see them. Early in the relationship, the passive partner helps the power partner hide insecurities and weaknesses. At an unconscious level, the passive partner needs the power partner to appear strong and capable. This illusion of strength and leadership fosters a false feeling of security and safety. The codependent grip tightens.

Later in the relationship, the passive partner recognizes some of the shortcomings of the power partner. Still yearning for security and safety, the passive partner is attracted to other people or groups where rigidity is operable, though in a seemingly more attractive and productive manner. Usually, there is hope that the passive partner's needs will be fully met by this new way of living the power-passive life-style. Both the power partner and the passive partner unconsciously see rigidity as the glue holding their frayed lives together.

The Lesson of Unity and Diversity

The same process that influences the power-passive relationship affects Christianity in a larger manner. If I may draw from the particular to the general, rigidity in its many forms is a present-day threat to relationships and to vibrant, functional Christian living.

Where is Christian art? Our present Christian environment doesn't readily promote such things as art, creativity, spontaneity, and freedom of thought. When Christians choose to limit their God-given freedoms, such things as art and self-expression naturally suffer. They may be seen as selfish, ungodly, and secular. We are created in God's image, who through an act of divine creativity created all that exists. Thus, we, too, are inbred with creativity. Certainly, we are to guard and defend the purity of our faith. But too often this role of defender of purity becomes only a justified excuse for continuance of rigidity.

Additionally, having thoughts that don't seem to fit in with the current Christian mind-set or having thoughts that question God or faith is close to blasphemy! I'm not talking about any form of heresy. I'm talking only about the right to think. For example, power persons may view legitimate developmental questions about the faith as heretical rather than as faith stretching. The field of Christian apologetics is not just for defending the faith to nonbelievers; it is for building up and encouraging the faith of believers. We can rejoice that we are on very solid and defensible ground.

I'm also referring to the fact that we feel things, even though we try to hide the emotions that we decide are inappropriate or embarrassing. Not long ago, two of our dearest friends lost their newborn child. I confessed to God that I was mad at Him. I knew I shouldn't be mad, but I felt mad just the same. I confessed that my anger blocked me from fully appreciating His love, grace, and kindness in the seemingly tragic situation. God clearly understood my feelings and graciously allowed me to work through them to a restored relationship with Him. Christ couldn't have repaired the damaged relationship had I denied my real feelings. Yet I know from my counseling experience that many well-meaning Christians, often drawing from Job, admonish struggling believers to stuff their feelings toward God as the negative emotions are deemed inappropriate. In a situation such as mine, I was not at all defying or questioning God. Rather, I was confessing my feelings and questioning my limited understanding of God. It is okay for Christians to do this. It may very well be sinful *not* to do this.

Praise God for biblical leaders throughout history who broke away from the chains of religious rigidity. Yet too many present-day believers allow someone else to do their thinking for them. That is especially true of the passive-dependent personality who, tiring of dependence on the rigid mate, may fall prey to cults or well-meaning Christian leaders who dictate how to live even in areas where their knowledge or experience may be incorrect, misinformed, or harmful. But the power partner is also drawn to structure and form as things unto themselves. Structure alone seduces the power partner by appealing to deeper emotional needs.

Professor Richard Rank, my graduate school friend and chairman of my dissertation committee, began his group theory and counseling course in an unusual way. His graduate students would assemble in a large room, anticipating his lecture to begin the course. Instead, he left the room. After twenty or thirty minutes, the students slowly realized that he had left and wasn't coming back. You can probably imagine the shock and dismay that went through the classroom. The students didn't know what to do, and they began to get visibly and verbally frustrated and upset. Several became quite angry! They seemed to react like drug addicts beginning withdrawal. Something they relied heavily upon had been taken away from them.

In the following class, Dr. Rank explained what had happened and unveiled the lesson behind the previous class experience. He challenged the students that they had become so acclimated to high levels of structure, they really didn't know what to do when little structure was provided. They had forgotten how to think and feel for themselves. They had become dependent and, perhaps, lazy.

They naturally expected someone else to lead them. They were used to being influenced and directed by authority figures and had almost become addicted to the routine, accepting leadership and teaching without thought and responsibility of their own. At the time of the class experience, some had become quite anxious; some had just waited; some had become hostile; others had seemed confused. Eventually, some individuals began to take initiative. Small groups of students assembled. They discussed the apparent problem and formulated strategies for coping with the unusual situation. Dr. Rank explained that that was when the group course really began. How they handled the situation had taught them a valuable lesson in group process and group member experience.

I really do think that many Christians are worse off than those graduate students. We love structure and guidelines. But too often we become, perhaps unknowingly, enslaved to them. We unwittingly sacrifice our Christian freedom and lose balance and perspective. We let others think for us. We let others lead us too easily. We get lazy. We coast along. We get so comfortable that we neglect our compass and road map.

You need structure and freedom.

Christianity is always balanced. We are to be structured and disciplined but not at the total expense of Christian freedom.

Our Christian freedom allows us to smell the roses along the way. The New Testament speaks of this matter of Christian freedom (see Rom. 6:18; 8:2; Gal. 3:28; 5:1). It may be thought of as liberty within boundaries, freedom with obedience. Christians are declared free from the slavery of sin through Christ's death. This freedom allows such things as creativity, beauty, expression, and the fruit of the Spirit while we simultaneously submit to Christ's authority, His Word, and His love. It allowed David to sing and dance in the streets while recognizing God's authority and supremacy. It's not all or nothing—one or the other—but liberty, celebration, and discovery *plus* obedience, discipline, and submission.

There are unity and diversity within the Trinity. The concept of the Trinity is hard enough to comprehend, but it is especially difficult for the power partner who primarily sees things as one way or the other—not two seemingly different things operating at the same time. And the Trinity is three persons and one at the same time! This concept requires thought. It is okay for Christians to use their minds.

There definitely are areas in Christianity where we should be stubbornly narrow (e.g., the virgin birth, the inerrancy of Scripture, etc.), but there are also areas where much freedom and creativity are allowed (e.g., time of day for prayer and Bible study, which Bible translation to use, etc.). There is a balance to maintain.

As with too many American-model Christians of the nineties, the power partner and the passive partner mistakenly confuse authoritarianism and inflexibility with discipline and freedom. Since everything is either black or white, life is all one way or its opposite. The notion of balanced Christianity has become muddied and obscure. Unity is confused with uniformity. Veiled rigidity is believed to be the norm for the Christian life. As a result, Christian art form and expression become connect-the-dots: "Just tell me what to do; I don't want to have to really think for myself. Give me a leader who worships rigidity, and I'll follow that person anywhere. Just tell me what I need to pass the course. I'm not really interested in learning.''

If the leader is correct in some helpful theological areas, rigid and passive-dependent persons swallow everything else without closely scrutinizing it all through God's Word plus wise and educated Christian counsel. The power partner is seduced by the appearance of structure, rules, authoritarianism, and form. These psychological enticements lay the groundwork for unquestioned fidelity. They feel familiar, so allegiance is given. The passive partner is seduced by the appearance of a benevolent caretaker that allows continued dependency. This psychological enticement lays the groundwork for unquestioned loyalty. Such blindspots and allurements mask biblical truth, which may be forfeited for psychological fulfillment, or protection, in the name of spirituality.

The passive partner marries to be taken care of. Initially, the power partner appears to fill the bill nicely. When the relationship begins to sour, the passive partner is easy prey for other rigid influences that seductively promise to provide what the rigid life-style or relationship has not.

Because of passive-dependency, the passive partner sacrifices personal needs, expression, feelings, growth, and thinking. This is not the kind of sacrifice the Lord desires. The passive partner must take full responsibility for the plight. The power partner must overcome rigidity in all its various forms. The challenges and warnings of this chapter are formidable and foreboding. The following chapter discusses key issues for the passive partner in overcoming the power-passive destruction.

Chapter 9

KEY ISSUES FOR THE PASSIVE PARTNER

Sherry was in the third grade, and all her classmates knew she was quiet. They teased her about it, calling her Shy Sherry. Sherry was shy, but she couldn't stand being teased about it. The teasing made her fear of humiliation and rejection worsen. Sherry knew that she needed to do something or she would keep being ridiculed.

Sherry finally summoned up enough courage to risk taking a bold initiative. She reasoned that she could dispel her classmates' kidding and gain new respect if she could come up with a good showing in front of her classmates. She would come up with an intelligent question to ask in front of everyone, designed to reveal her heretofore hidden abilities. Surely, she reasoned, her classmates would then learn new respect and appreciation for her. She was very nervous about it. She had never done anything like that before. But she was determined her plan must work.

One early morning just before the lesson started, Sherry's hand shot straight up. Her teacher, being taken somewhat off guard, though pleasantly interested, inquired what Sherry wanted. With newfound confidence and a somewhat shaky voice, Sherry asked, "Just who is this Richard Stands anyway?" Her teacher responded, "I beg your pardon?" By then, Sherry was feeling a degree of confidence since her teacher seemed to be somewhat dumbfounded. All of her classmates had turned toward her and were listening attentively. Sherry could feel her stomach twisting into knots as she continued. "Richard Stands," she repeated, "exactly who is he?" "I'm not sure I understand," replied her teacher. "You know," Sherry continued, "every morning when we say the pledge of allegiance, we end up by saying, 'And to the public for Richard Stands.' "

Her classmates paused for a moment and then screamed hysterically with laughter. Even her teacher could not hold back a restrained smirk. The very thing Sherry was trying to overcome (her fear of humiliation and rejection) was rudely intensified by the experience. Sherry never spoke up again. She resolved that she would never be so humiliated and rejected again. A passive partner was born that morning. Thirty years later, she was still the same way. She needed professional counseling. Her passive-dependency had cost her much. It also cost Sherry her marriage.

Delivery from Dependency—Desooner, Debetter

The passive partner life-style just doesn't work. It didn't work for Sherry, it won't work for you, and it isn't biblical. The best wimp is an ex-wimp.

There are some tough barriers to hurdle to end the passive-dependent life-style. Don't expect help from your mate. The power partner will fight you every step of the way, not realizing that your change is the best thing for both partners. Don't be surprised if some close friends or family members won't help, either. They have gotten used to you in your award-winning role of nice guy. They get a lot of mileage out of you, too. But fear not. Some of us will stick by you and help you dewimp.

Let's not fool ourselves. Dewimping is going to be a major project. Your cholesterol level has been found to be over three hundred, so you've got to completely alter your diet, lose weight, exercise, and so on. This analogy is not too far off since dewimping requires a change of heart and a change of life-style. You can't be patched up. You need a complete overhaul that lasts. This chapter addresses key tasks involved in your overhaul. This chapter talks about *what* needs to be done. The following chapter addresses an equally important subject: *how* to go about doing it.

Holding the Trump Card

As might have been expected, Sherry grew up and married a power partner. The marriage ended after twelve years of power-passive patterns of relating. Sherry believed that the answer to the problems in her marriage was to become a better passive partner (rather than learn how not to be a passive partner at all). It didn't work. She never realized that she held the trump card all along.

Holding the trump card meant that Sherry had more power and influence in the relationship than she recognized. But she didn't know how to use it to help, and finally to save, her relationship. She could have given her husband what he really needed: control and power in the relationship *if and when* he chose to lead in a biblical manner that was relationally responsible and psychologically sound.

---

*Passive partners must learn
loving firmness.*

The passive partner must learn to exercise loving firmness. Such Christ-centered toughness should not be confused with anger or bitterness. It is the message: "I love you very much, but you're not going to push me around anymore or abuse me in any way. This isn't good for me or for you. I'm not going to hurt you. I'm going to love you as Christ works in me to effect loving behaviors that I may not feel at the moment. Do not mistake my confidence and conviction for resistance. Do not mistake my zeal to submit to God or your mistaken concept of biblical submission as license to walk all over me. And do not be surprised when I stand up for God and for myself!"

The passive partner (passive-dependent personality and/or passive marital role) must learn to overcome

- lack of awareness of the power partner's games and strategies for the relationship.
- power struggles.
- lack of awareness of one's own strengths and position in the relationship.
- false forgiveness, lack of tolerance, anger, and resentment.
- misinterpretation of Scripture and misunderstanding by well-meaning Christian peers and leaders.
- lack of self-confidence, the inability to stand up for self, and unbiblical self-neglect.
- passivity disguised as niceness or Christian virtue.
- dependency fears associated with threats of desertion, humiliation, abandonment, isolation, aloneness, and rejection.
- false feelings of guilt, wrongdoing, responsibility, obligation, or inadequacy.
- reluctance to build outside support systems, lack of accountability, and reluctance to seek and maintain support and/or professional help.
- loss of touch or distortion of feelings.
- mistaken notions of love and intimacy.

Power-Passive Games

Definitive and predictable games occur in power-passive relationships. I hesitate to use the word *game* due to the seriousness of the interpersonal transaction and its effects on the individuals involved and the codependent relationship itself. However, the term is useful in considering the relational activities that have as a goal the maintenance of the codependent relationship with the power partner in the superior, and destructive, position. The goal for the power partner is to maintain control of the relationship and to continue to gainfully employ all of the preeminence of the power partner life-style. The goal of the passive partner is to not suffer the consequences of personal fears while placating the mate.

Twelve basic games are played. There are variations on each, and other games may be attempted. These twelve, though, almost always work. Of course, not all power-passive relationships rely on all twelve games, but every relationship is capable of each game at some time. The more dysfunctional the codependent relationship has become, the more likely that most of the games have been used. Or in dysfunctional dyads, one or two may be frequently employed with a high degree of regularity. The passive partner who recognizes these games can refuse to get suckered into them. The twelve key games, or "the dirty dozen," are as follows:

1. *The Superiority Game*. For Christians, this can also become the "Holier Than Thou" Game. The idea is that the power partner is presented as smarter, brighter, more educated (in whatever area), more experienced, more spiritual, and so on. Hence, it is reasoned, due to such impeccable qualifications and abilities, the power partner gets to make all the important decisions regardless of the mate's input (or anyone else's input). The power partner is the self-appointed authority, a legend in his own mind.

Submission works both ways. God's design is for both parties to complement, enhance, and consummate each other. Either party would be foolish to neglect input from the other. The priest of the family is ultimately accountable for the final decision, but he is equally responsible to be a wise steward and to cultivate input from his spouse. In some, perhaps many, areas, she may be the actual expert.

The passive partner should seize the opportunity to study up on an issue with a goal of contributing positively to the mutual decision-making process. If the passive partner does well in a few selected areas, presenting a documented view in a well-thought-out and rational manner, the power partner will learn to respect and appreciate input in other areas as well.

2. *The Comptroller Controller Game.* The power partner becomes the royal household official who examines and controls all household expenditures. This comptroller controls the money. The passive partner is treated like staff.

An old Chinese saying goes something like this: "He who has the fattest wallet sits tallest." The power partner understands this principle. The passive partner may need to demonstrate competence in smaller areas to gain the mate's confidence in larger areas. The goal is to show competence that can make the power partner look good rather than pose a threat. The goal for the power partner is to help the mate develop confidence in the ability to handle the situation (in this case, money matters) to appreciate the mate's present abilities in a spirit of trust and responsibility while recognizing the wrong motivation for needing to control the situation.

3. *The Divide and Conquer Game.* The power partner tries to prevent the passive-dependent mate from gaining support systems outside the relationship. The power partner unconsciously wants the passive partner isolated and alone. The power partner wants to be the sole influence on the passive partner's life and finds ways to ward off the competition.

Spiritual and emotional support are as necessary as food and water. The passive partner is still a vital part of the body of Christ who needs to receive ministering as well as to minister to the body. The prison door is opened wide. Yet sometimes the passive partner sits and stares as if it were locked tight.

4. *The Look How Well I Treat You Game.* This game is designed to teach the passive partner not to make waves in the relationship and to divert attention from problematic areas with constant reminders of how good things are. This game is also

played in front of others to create or maintain a positive image of the power partner.

The passive partner's role is to recognize the positive things the rigid mate does but not overlook problem areas. If the power partner has to announce, brag, or merchandise kindness, it automatically terminates and retracts the act of benevolence and becomes manipulation.

5. *The Emotional Blackmail Game.* The power partner plays on the fears of the passive partner, especially the fears of abandonment, isolation, aloneness, desertion, and rejection. The power partner finds ways to remind the passive partner of the great distress and inescapable failure that would be experienced apart from their relationship.

The passive partner needs to be prepared to prove that, though there is no desire for it to happen, the passive partner can make it alone if it comes to that! Once such ability is demonstrated, this particular game is terminated.

6. *The Big Boss Game.* The power partner likes to engage in power struggles. Power struggles are transactions designed to ascertain who really is in control. The power partner likes to be the big boss.

Sidestep power struggles.

The passive partner must learn to recognize when a power struggle is brewing and sidestep it altogether. A big boss without someone to boss isn't a boss at all. It takes two to make a power struggle. It's okay to encourage good leadership. The power partner needs to remember that real leadership comes from within, not from without.

7. *The Submission Game.* The power partner gets a lot of mileage out of this game. It's a disguised version of the Big Boss Game. By distorting biblical passages on submission, the power partner can dictate terms and can feel "saintly" while doing it!

The passive partner may want to reread chapters 3 and 6 as they address the misuse and abuse of submission. Constant reminders of these "submit or die" passages indicate the power partner's motivation is probably wrong. If, however, the power partner lives out servant-leadership, it becomes easy to do likewise. It becomes something done out of love and appreciation.

8. *The Wrecked Sex Game*. In this clever variation of the Submission Game, the "biblically versed" power partner uses Scripture to subjugate the spouse in the area of sex. The information is used to force the spouse into being "obedient" or "Christian." The passive partner feels something is very wrong, yet reluctantly yields due to misinformation.

The power partner needs to learn to understand sex from the passive partner's perspective and then seek to use this knowledge tenderly, passionately, and compassionately in the love-making process. If that happens, rewards will be forthcoming.

9. *The Leader versus Dictator Game*. Saddam Hussein called his captives "guests" while President Bush was correct in calling them "hostages." The dictator was trying to appear as a leader. The power partner resembles a dictator more than a servant-leader. Robing himself in Christian garb, the designated priest of the family confuses spiritual appointment with worldly entitlement. He instructs his mate and others to perform duties and tasks according to self-interests. He is a leader who needs to be served rather than a servant-leader.

10. *The Confusion Game*. Dr. Milton Erickson, the famous psychiatrist and expert on the unconscious mind, was driving down a busy street. As he stopped at an intersection, a group of tough-looking motorcyclists drove up beside him. For no apparent reason, they looked over at Dr. Erickson and began calling him names and insulting him. Dr. Erickson leaned over, rolled down his window, looked right at them, and said, "I'm ugly, too!" As the ruffians were still scratching their heads in confusion, Dr. Erickson calmly rode off down the road without further incident. He used the confusion technique to completely disarm them while he drove safely away.

The Confusion Game is similar to what happened in that scenario. The power partner tries to confuse the mate. The passive partner begins to doubt self and relinquishes whatever progress was being made. The focus is on employing means to knock the passive partner off stride. This diversion tactic works well since the passive partner easily accepts blame even when it doesn't apply anyway. If there is some question about what has happened, or things appear vague, the passive partner falsely assumes responsibility. In so doing, the passive partner also undermines the developing triune self-concept and loses momentum. The passive partner begins to doubt self, thereby forcing increased dependence on the power partner. Presto—the power partner's back in control again!

When the passive partner begins to feel confused, especially on a continuing basis, the passive partner should sound the alarm and recognize what is happening. The power partner must not allow confusion to occur. If it does, the power partner must act promptly to clear up matters in a way that enlightens the mate.

11. *The Blame Game*. The power partner takes advantage of the passive partner's hair-trigger acceptance of wrongdoing by shifting the focus onto the passive partner. There are two basic versions: (1) "Oh, yeah? Well, you are worse than I am"; and (2) "Oh, yeah? Well, let's talk about something else you do poorly."

Neither party should blindly accept blame. Both parties should be quick to own up to their part of the problem. Each person must carefully examine what has occurred with the goal of quickly, cooperatively, and efficiently mending the problem.

12. *The Swindler (or Manipulation) Game*. This game comes in assorted sizes and colors. In the "switch the subject" version, the power partner changes the topic of conversation when responsibility begins to point at the power partner. In the "guilt tripper," the power partner uses tactics designed to make the mate surrender the position due to feelings of assumed or implied culpability or wrongdoing. In the "lobbyer" version,

the power partner goes to various constituents of the relationship to try to persuade them to see things as the power partner does and to vote against the mate.

Each version of this game involves gaining unfair advantage through dishonest means or through unfair emotional methods. Each involves using the passive partner's feelings against self to win an argument or to gain advantage for a held belief or position. There is no place for manipulation, by either party, in any healthy relationship.

The Weakness of the Power Struggle

There is a distorted perceptual process in the power-passive relationship. What seems to be useful in coping with the pressures of the relationship is not usually helpful at all.

Power struggles are weak because they don't work in relationships. A power struggle is an ongoing battle to demonstrate who is in charge. Since power partners are so insecure, they need constant assurance that ultimate control is theirs. Hence they engage in power struggles, often employing one of the power-passive games, to remind themselves that the world is running the way they need it to run. Passive partners really don't want to be in charge but end up in power struggles due to anger and resentment of the bullying and abuse of the continual battles.

Agree to follow Christ's will.

Both parties need to learn to recognize power struggles and to avoid them. A viable alternative is to constantly recognize that neither is in charge and to actively agree to come together to determine and to follow Christ's will for every situation. Where there are gray areas, where Christ's will is unclear, or where there is freedom to choose, each member needs to resolve to submit to the other. It is an acceptable decision for each party to choose something different. Once one member begins considering the other's feelings ahead of personal feelings, the individual leads the way for the mate to do likewise. Then the relationship has the capability to be constituted of two givers rather than two takers.

Dead-End Street

Betty Littler had run the course with her rigid mate, becoming burned out, deenergized, and defeated. She confided to me that she had secretly been seeing another man. She knew it was wrong, but she had no intention of calling it off. She had grown to resent her marriage, and her nonsexual affair was a passive way of showing resistance and anger.

Her husband, Gil, had recently purchased a new car without including Betty in the decision (Leader versus Dictator). He explained that the vehicle was on loan as a demonstrator, but he intended to buy it later that week. Betty explained that she thought their financial picture didn't allow for such a purchase, especially since her household allowance was already so meager (Comptroller Controller).

Gil insisted that it would be a reasonable buy and cited various considerations for buying it that Betty couldn't appreciate (Superiority). After only a few days, Gil had worn her down, making her feel selfish for depriving him of such a purchase. After all he'd done for her over the past years (e.g., nice home, place to sleep, etc.), Betty began to believe she was genuinely in his debt (Look How Well I Treat You). Betty did what she usually did: succumbed due to feelings of guilt (Swindler).

Gil won the battle. He got his new car. He couldn't understand why Betty couldn't seem to put the whole matter behind her after the purchase. Betty couldn't put the matter behind her, though, and she couldn't understand why she couldn't. She learned that it wasn't one episode she was reacting to. Rather, it was the pattern that the episode represented. That pattern was the life-style of the power-passive relationship.

Betty learned that she was on a dead-end street. Every option she had was a losing option. Her depression affirmed that losing feeling—even though her mind couldn't figure it out. She felt guilty for the wrong reason. Betty felt guilty because she was having an affair. She was indeed guilty. Gil had tried to make her feel guilty, but that particular guilt was based on false guilt. He was unaware of the affair. Betty couldn't contest or fight the false guilt due to the true guilt she felt from her sinful behavior. So she wimped out, but she became increasingly resentful of the destructive pattern, directing her anger at Gil in a passive manner. The power-passive pattern had made her susceptible to the affair and had indirectly prolonged it.

Betty was able to call off her affair because she was able to see her no-win situation. In therapy, she reasoned that by doing so she would no longer have to experience false guilt. She could begin to stand up for herself and to stand against the destructive power-passive relationship. The focus of her relational problems could be shifted onto the real problem of the power-passive relationship. Obviously, extramarital affairs are wrong and sinful. If that is not bad enough, affairs are self-defeating in that they don't allow the passive-dependent member to grow out of the dysfunction. Jumping into another relationship, no matter how attractive it may appear, only allows the difficulties of the original passive-dependency, or the troubles of the original rigidity, to disable another relationship with new forms of problems that are at least as difficult as the previous ones. If a race car has engine trouble, the solution is not to go to another track. A tune-up or an overhaul is necessary before other avenues even need to be considered.

False Guilt and Shooting Christians

Betty's true guilt masked the problem of her false guilt. False guilt arises many times in the power-passive relationship. The power partner is adept at using the Swindler Game, and the passive partner is too quick to accept unwarranted blame.

Additionally, the passive partner often has to dodge the bullets of shooting Christians who, in a well-meaning manner, wound the passive-dependent individual due to quick, or inaccurate, judgments based on misinformation, misunderstanding, and misguided mandates or expectations. Job's friends were examples of such admonishers. Such "help" causes the passive partner to feel more guilty (false guilt), misunderstood, and defeated. The passive partner usually interprets the feelings of false guilt to be true guilt because well-meaning Christians have so declared it. The well-meaning, but naive, Christian "helper" thereby takes on the role of the power partner.

Often, the power partner manipulates such "helpers" to join in the conflict to strengthen an unbiblical position. The passive partner needs to remember that true guilt is not determined by popular vote. Neither is it determined by misinformed Christians, pastors, or counselors. Ultimately, the passive partner has to answer only to Jesus. So do they. I'm not at all saying to ignore or disregard these people. I am, however, cautioning the passive partner to be careful and cautious in determining true versus false guilt, and right versus wrong actions, and to be selective and discerning in deciding who to listen to as well as what to believe. There are rigid people in Christian clothing, in pastors' robes, in counseling offices, and in other "expert" roles.

Love Limits

Love is paradoxical. It is boundless yet contains necessary limits. The greatest and most sublime demonstration of love (see John 3:16) contained limits. Love limits do not imply conditional love. We are to love unconditionally while maintaining biblical limits. Such a concept is easily recognized and appreciated if we consider our children. Our love contains limits: "Yes, I love you, but no, you can't play in the street!" It is not so easily recognized when it comes to our mate or to ourselves. It is especially difficult for the passive-dependent spouse to set and maintain limits that are necessary to preserve biblical dignity in the relationship.

No More Mr. Nice Guy

Jesus died for you. You are an inestimable prize to Him. He died for power and passive people alike. Because of who He is, and because of His love for us, we have real worth. When we feel that we aren't worth much, the feeling is certainly not from God. The apostle Paul warns Christians about using the wrong measuring stick in evaluating ourselves (see 2 Cor. 10:12). Of course, if we are sinning and living in disobedience, we should feel poorly. But our worth comes from Him even when we sin. Our ability to feel and experience that worth is affected by our level of obedience and by our sin nature, which shrouds our means of accurately evaluating ourselves. That doesn't mean if we walk with Christ, we'll be happy all the time and only good things will happen to us. But we'll have feelings that are biblically appropriate to who we are and to our life experiences.

In chapter 3, we saw that Jesus was not passive. He taught us balance: to stand up for ourselves in the appropriate situations and to be submissive in the appropriate situations. We know that Jesus was not a rigid person, either. He certainly was dogmatic about the appropriate things, but He also was flexible and open-minded about things. One could say that He drank wine, went to the wrong places, and hung out with the wrong people. From a rigid perspective, all that looks pretty bad. At least, he could have done a better job with His public relations image.

Jesus was careful about His image for His Father's sake. But He didn't let it keep Him from living a godly life. In today's society, we Christians are careful of our image, too. And we should be. But there is a balance. We must be careful. Every church community is not going to understand the situation of the passive partner. Nor is every local church going to fully understand some of the tough things a passive-dependent person is going to have to do to follow Christ. From the outside, the passive partner may seem to be disobedient when the person is not. These same people would probably have rebuked Jesus for doing things that they deemed ''non-Christian''!

And some of these same people are going to be royally fooled by the power partner, who will look like the good guy when the person is not. The passive partner will look like the good guy only when allowing the rigid mate to be rigid while ''submissively'' complying with the passive partner role. This process, however, is unbiblical and psychologically destructive.

Be nice but tough!

The passive partner must adapt an attitude of no more Mr. Nice Guy. In actuality, the passive partner is still being nice—just nice and tough!

Send for the Cavalry

There will be people who will love the passive partner through this ordeal and who will understand what's happening. At the very least, the passive partner needs to have folks praying for both partners and for the marriage. The passive partner must be discreet about how to obtain prayer so as not to ignite the power partner.

If the power-passive marriage has become a problem (this usually happens over time to mid-range couples, and definitely is already occurring to severe dyads), notify the pastor, and if the situation has become severe, consider taking it before the church leadership. This process is usually initiated by the passive partner with varying degrees of reluctance from the power partner.

At various points in this book, the passive-dependent spouse's eyes are opened to more clearly recognize the rigidity of the mate. Such a realization (and subsequent feelings of violation) may occur several times throughout the healing process. It may lead to subsequent hasty decisions and anger-driven reactions that will be directed toward the power partner. Christ-dependency, self-control, and patience will continue to be of vital importance through the entire process of individual and relational change.

I hope that both members will be agreeable to getting help. You may choose to seek out a reputable and well-credentialed Christian counselor. Be careful who you see because some Christian counseling approaches are rigid and will only worsen matters. You don't want to see a counselor who pulls out a Bible and orders the passive partner to submit! I would recommend a Christian counselor who has been trained in both theological and psychological methods of understanding problems and relationships. The person should have adequate training (e.g., graduate level study and/or degrees) and experience in both areas. Such individuals are highly trained, and they are not likely to be rigid. A qualified helper who isn't rigid can understand the passive partner's confused, angered, distorted, or lost feelings and can assist the passive partner with understanding and overcoming mistaken notions of love and intimacy.

False Forgiveness

One task of the power partner is to ask forgiveness for the way the rigidity has affected the passive-dependent mate. Simply wanting to forgive someone, or saying the words, however, does not mean that forgiveness has occurred. There are also times when the passive partner really does want to forgive the mate and believes it has happened—but it has not. Forgiveness is especially difficult when the power partner keeps on being rigid, though to a lesser degree, in certain areas without meaning to do so.

Just as there is cheap grace, there is also cheap forgiveness. Such forgiveness has occurred prematurely, artificially, or superficially.

Remember Gil and Betty Littler? Only one week after having purchased his new car against Betty's wishes, Gil told her that her "problem" was that she couldn't put things behind her and she needed to forgive him. Then she could move forward in the relationship. But she could not.

Gil needed to recognize that his pressure on Betty to forgive was representative of the power partner's life-style. Such a request was another form of rigidity and a new type of abuse. How could anyone completely forgive someone who was still committing the same misdeed?

In such a power-passive situation, forgiveness must be a process. It was wrong and insensitive for Gil to think Betty could turn off such feelings and reactions. He should not expect that to happen immediately.

Betty might have responded, "I do want to forgive you. I want to put this recent episode behind us. You are right that there's no use crying over spilled milk; however, that's not really the case here. I am feeling pressured to do something, again, that I'm not sure I'm quite ready to do yet. It's this bigger pattern that my emotions are reacting to. Please give me more time, and please don't put additional pressures on me. I love you."

It would be nice if Bill responded, "I was wrong to push you. I didn't even realize that I was doing it. I'm working hard to change. I don't want our destructive pattern to continue. I love you far too much for that. Please continue to help me see the things I do that hurt you when I'm not aware of them. I won't question your right to feel the way that you do. I'll work hard at not putting pressures on you. Of course, I'll give you more time. Please give me more time, too. I love you." The constant prayer of the couple is, "Lord, please deliver us from the rigidity and passive-dependency destroying our relationship. Help us to follow You. Help us to model You in our transactions with each other. Help us to pursue the triune model while overcoming all the negative aspects of our codependent relationship."

This chapter has examined some of the tough tasks a passive partner faces in overcoming the destructive power-passive dynamic. It has addressed the what-to-do's of handling the relationship. However, it's not just *what* the couple does but *how* the couple goes about it. If the power partner and the passive partner follow these guidelines in a cooperative manner, the relationship is well on the way to healing. The next chapter addresses the how-to part—how to go about making the changes outlined in this chapter and throughout this book.

Chapter 10

THE HOW-TO'S OF NECESSARY CHANGE

When power partners or passive partners decide that they are ready for change, they will find that change is not going to be very easy at all. There will be all kinds of things working against successful transformation. Even with the cooperation of the mate, efforts will be sabotaged, criticized, fought, and resisted in various ways. In the power-passive scheme of things, power partners have the advantage in the codependent relationship. Most things work out to their favor. So expect the power partner to resist needed change in the functioning of the relationship. The mild power partner (mild rigidity) will try to cooperate but will likely, perhaps unconsciously, resist it. The mid-range power partner (moderate rigidity) will agree to change in principle but will fight it unconsciously and consciously. The severe power partner (severe rigidity) will fight it every step of the way.

The how-to's of real change require two integral steps: (1) recognition and ownership of the problem, and (2) subsequent alteration of behaviors and responsibilities, within one's power, that lead to successful transformation. Recognition of a problem is complicated by denial, which is a major obstacle to genuine change. I have marveled at certain members of the sample power-passive group of clients who, having read the material in this book, consistently minimize their degree of symptoms and participation in power-passivity. Even obviously severe partners classify themselves as mild. This self-evaluation contains obvious elements of denial, but admittedly, any admission and confession is better than none. For the Christian, personal responsibility is accompanied by the internal dwelling of the Holy Spirit who empowers change and gently illumines truth.

The passive-dependent mate really doesn't want that much change either due to codependent needs. The need for change is realized, but there is fear about the process of change. Thus, two fairly contentious cohorts are working to produce needed change that neither fully wants. What a mess!

If, however, the relationship has begun its downward spiral, one or both members may be quite ready for change. It's not really a question of whether or not either spouse wants to change. They are commanded to change by God. We are to become holy. We are to become like Christ. That is impossible in the power-passive, codependent relationship. Change is mandated, and it is the only real option.

The power and the passive partners are like porcupines. When the two porcupines decided what they wanted to do, they found that it was fairly easy to get right to the point with each other. However, when they wanted to hug each other, they discovered the how-to hug part was a rather prickly situation. Just how did they do it? Very carefully!

The changes needed for both partners have been previously addressed. The what-to-do's have been discussed in some detail. The how-to-do's are equally important. It's not just knowing that we've got to get the football into the end zone that wins the game. There have to be strategies, and there have to be ways of employing the strategies. Similarly, there are strategies for changing the power-passive relationship. Like our porcupine friends, however, these how-to's need to be approached very carefully.

The Need for Demonstrated Respect

As Christians, you and your mate are commanded to love each other (see John 13:34; 15:1–27; Eph. 4:2, 32; Gal. 5:22). Behaving in love involves being respectful, considerate, trustworthy, and giving to your mate. As you act lovingly and Christlike toward your mate, your emotions follow along. You can literally act your way to new, or renewed, feelings toward your mate. This acting does not mean pretending. It means loving your mate out of your love, obedience, and respect to Christ—even when the positive, associative feelings may be lacking.

Communicate respect for your mate.

A primary strategy for overcoming the power-passive dysfunction involves communicating respect for each other as you and your mate go about the process of undoing the power-passive codependency. Breaking this cycle is going to be hard enough without further alienating your mate at the same time. Relational respect is a necessary ingredient for maintaining the dignity of both parties. Even when each member is disagreeing, or disengaging, there should continue to be communicated respect for the value of the other person. That respect doesn't mean you give in to the other person's demands when the requests are ungodly. It does mean that, even in the face of change or resistance, respect for the other person is maintained.

It's the "love the sinner, hate the sin" approach. You are to keep on loving and respecting your mate even when the person engages in sinful behavior or makes ungodly demands on you. That doesn't mean, at all, that you budge one iota on the what-to part. Rather, you carefully communicate your love for the sinner while you refuse to engage in sinful demands, requests, or behaviors. When you are placed in the position of having to be obedient to your mate or to God, you always choose the latter, praying your mate can adjust to it, and doing all that you can to be sure that you clearly understand God's will and that your mate also receives adequate opportunity to truthfully grasp God's directives.

The quality of a marriage can be measured by the degree of sensitivity and respect between the mates. The power-passive relationship suffers from lack of sensitivity and respect. Below is a list of ten vital components for building mutual respect into your marriage.

The Ten Commandments of Marital Respect

1. *Respect each other's feelings.* At the heart of disrespect is the message, stated or implied, "You don't count." Feelings are valid subjective experiences by an individual, which reflect the inner world and affect self-esteem. By sharing feelings, your mate is revealing an intimate part of life. Work toward being open, vulnerable, and honest with each other about your feelings and viewpoints. It is important to communicate that all feelings are legitimate. Never say, "You shouldn't feel that way." You don't have to understand or to agree with the other person's feelings, but you do need to esteem and honor those feelings. After you have demonstrated that it's okay to have feelings, you can work on understanding them better and possibly changing them if change is appropriate.

2. *Respect each other's worth.* Value and esteem each other, treating the believing spouse as precious personal property of the Lord of lords. God gave His beloved Son to die on the cross for us. He didn't do this because of any intrinsic merit or good deed on our part. He did it because of His love for us and to reconcile us to Himself. Abundantly sublime and ultimate expression and validation of our worth are in this spiritual truth.

You must also look for ways to express appreciation and acknowledgment of the things that your mate gives to you—from parenting to ironing to changing the oil to turning out the lights at night. Say how much you appreciate the big and little things your mate does.

3. *Respect each other's thoughts*. This doesn't mean you have to agree with every thought so much as you must honor your mate's ability to think and reason. Realize that your mate may see things differently from the way you do. If both thought the same way and did things the same way all of the time, one of you would be unnecessary. God gave you each other to complete oneness—to complement and to enhance each other. Don't see your mate's different point of view as threatening or disrespectful; see it as complementary and enhancing. Encourage your mate to utilize and continually develop the mind. See the mental capabilities as a family asset.

4. *Respect each other's actions*. Don't be too quick to criticize, judge, or condemn. Conform your behavior to what Christ would do in your situation. Persevere with each other even at times when things don't outwardly look or feel too great. In the long run such steadfastness builds trust and establishes faithfulness. Remember also that actions speak louder than words. Your mate will hear what you do more clearly than what you say. Be sure your words are backed up consistently by your actions.

5. *Respect each other's abilities*. Look to build up each other and to encourage growth and good works rather than to discourage, frustrate, or lose heart with each other. Learn to be satisfied with the abilities that exist rather than to be frustrated about the abilities not found. Never exclude your mate from any decisions, actions, or feelings that affect the relationship. Try to include your mate in personal areas of decisions, actions, or feelings. That doesn't mean your mate dictates what will happen. That means your mate is actively recognized as being important and the feedback is valued and appreciated.

6. *Respect each other's giving of self*. Learn to be content with your mate's efforts at loving rather than be discontent about what you think you need. Continue to find new ways to give of yourself (without giving up yourself).

Preserve the dignity of the relationship by honoring and building each other's self-esteem. Lying underneath the pile of symptoms and characteristics of the power and passive partners is insecurity based on low self-esteem. Attacking the other person's self-esteem in any way will only worsen the symptoms. Look for ways to reward and encourage your mate as appropriate changes are sought. Learn to ignore slips into old, dysfunctional behaviors rather than to highlight them by negative attention or punishment.

Sometimes it is helpful to consider the sources of your deeper insecurities. Often, you can separate out the notion that your insecurity was not so much your defect as it was your reaction to your sinful nature coupled with living in the sinful world. Recognize such things as an overprotective parent, a parent who criticized, or family dysfunction (e.g., alcoholism, drugs, sexual or emotional abuse, etc.) as programming you for future difficulties, such as feeling inadequate and/or insecure and/or fearful. Once you begin to acknowledge such possibilities, you can start to create an awareness that leads to self-examination and self-confrontation that can produce change and victory. It then becomes a matter not of being lost in the middle of nowhere with no hope of getting out but of being temporarily disoriented with a road map and compass at your side. Again, the key here is to understand your own, and especially your mate's, behavioral symptoms as coming from deeper needs. These needs must be respected. The overt symptom may well be thought of as a cry for help, but to help, you must look beyond your immediate wants and need fulfillment to active ministry to your mate. Each is to seek to minister in such a manner.

7. *Respect each other's spiritual development.* Learn to encourage each other's spiritual growth; learn to grow together spiritually. Pray for each other. Pray with each other. See that your mate's, and your own, spiritual gifts and abilities are recognized, developed, and used. Maintain a devotional life. Study God's Word. Be involved with God's people.

8. *Respect each other's need for affection and intimacy.*

Learn to be affectionate and demonstrative of your genuine feelings of esteem, appreciation, satisfaction, desire, and love. Learn how to communicate at a deeper level. Make intimacy, or emotional, spiritual, and physical closeness, one of the highest priorities for your marriage. Work at listening to what your mate has to say in such a way that you communicate your mate's value and importance.

9. *Respect each other's relational loyalty and commitment.* Respect each other's loyalty and commitment to Christ and to each other. Even if you need to engage in tough love, realize that you are doing so out of your commitment to God and to your mate. Have as your commitment Christ, first; marriage, second; and then the rest. Nothing must get in the way of these two priorities.

10. *Respect each other's individual and relational responsibility.* Develop abilities to show care for each other; allow your mate to take responsibility for personal behavior; be a good steward of all God has given you; take ownership of your reactions, behaviors, beliefs, thoughts, and feelings without bringing your mate into it (e.g., by blaming, by being angry or disappointed, by comparing self versus mate, etc.). You can't change your mate. That's not your responsibility. You are responsible for yourself. You are responsible to Christ for what you do with every part of your life. You are to act to change the power-passive marriage with or without the help of your mate. If, for example, your mate doesn't want help or counseling, you are to get help and/or counseling for your part. Such help can include books, seminars, classes, self-help groups, peer support, church leadership, pastoral guidance, prayer support, professional counseling, and more.

The Costs of Incomplete Help

Lynn Lidder, a dear Christian woman who was a recognized church leader, came to see me for problems with a penetrating depression that she concealed from those around her. She could not let others see her struggle because she felt it was unbiblical and it would discourage others. As a leader, she felt especially burdened to overcome her emotional battle. She had tried numerous methods of dealing with her depression, including seeing four Christian counselors across several states over the past three years. She didn't realize that many Christian leaders— even Paul (see 2 Cor. 7:6–7)—struggled with depression and anxiety.

Lynn grew up in a dysfunctional home. Her father was very detached, critical, and demanding. Her mother was always discouraged, quiescent, and unaffectionate. Lynn never really felt loved. She always felt like she wasn't good enough. That was the message she learned in her home. She grew up in a power-passive family.

Lynn carried into adulthood the message learned in her family. She felt inadequate, insecure, and unlovable. Other people would never have guessed how she felt deep down inside. Outwardly, she exuded confidence and competence. What she learned as a child became a self-fulfilling prophecy as she continued to experience her world the same way as an adult. Though she was very skilled and professional, she worked for low wages. She lived in circumstances far below a woman of her stature. She resented her circumstances, and she felt guilty for resenting them. She let others constantly take advantage of her in every situation, believing it was the biblical way to act. Yet she resented others who treated her that way, and she felt guilty for her additional resentment.

Lynn told me that she was at the end of her rope. She wrestled with suicidal thoughts, and she rationalized that God would forgive her for such an ultimate ''solution'' to her problems. One counselor told her she needed to be more submissive and obedient, but that didn't seem to help. In fact, she resented the counsel and became more upset. Another counselor told her that she needed to experience her pain, but her pain was already making her suicidal, though she never told him that. Her distress was already causing her emotional anguish, and she wanted less, not more, of that. Another counselor suggested various Scriptures, recommended other readings, and prayed with her—but somehow those things didn't work, either. So Lynn felt even worse—and abandoned by God. Another tried studying and applying specific Scriptures with her, admonishing her to quit her sinful behavior. Lynn was supposed to give her problem to Christ. Since it was still there, she thought she must not have enough faith or she must not really be a committed Christian or she must be continuing in some other sinful behavior. The well-meaning approaches to help Lynn brought her to the brink of desperation and despair. Though there is some degree of merit in each approach, none of them was sufficient. She needed more.

There were psychological processes going on that had not really been considered. Lynn was a passive-dependent personality who felt inadequate and let others take unfair advantage of her. And her Christian friends were the worst ones! She was a pleaser who performed for others to gain emotional approval.

Lynn began studying and applying the principles and suggestions outlined in this book. She also began a process that revolutionized her life and eventually overcame her depression. She began standing up for herself, even though she didn't feel any sense of personal worth or merit. She began to realize that, even though she felt inadequate and worthless emotionally, she *was* adequate and worthwhile spiritually. After all, the God of the universe sent Lynn His most treasured and beloved possession. There is real, priceless, and ultimate worth because of Christ.

Act on truth, and feelings will follow.

Though she couldn't feel it, she believed the biblical truths. She then acted on the basis of her beliefs, despite her feelings to the contrary. The hope was that, as she began acting on the basis of her faith in God's Word, she would reap the benefits of real and ongoing change. The process starts off with change based on biblical truth and subsequent action (despite feelings), and then follows basic operant conditioning principles—the positive consequences of changed actions allow continued reinforced transformation.

Lynn learned to act assertively to gain acceptance and respect rather than await others' acceptance and respect in her passive-dependent role. At first, others resented her change. Lynn almost backed down from the necessary assertiveness that eventually earned her dignity and subsequent acceptance and respect. But she understood the dynamics, worked through the psychological blocks, and persevered to break the self-defeating cycle she had maintained all her life.

Standing Up for Assertiveness

The same way of thinking that concludes that there's no such thing as self-esteem for the Christian because the concept itself is selfish also concludes that there's no such thing as assertiveness, either. The terms *self-esteem* and *self-concept*, however, are not so much new discoveries, or secular propaganda, as they are descriptors for how we regard, esteem, and conceptualize ourselves: our personhood; our being; our value; our worth; our meaning; our existence. It takes a lot of self-esteem to say there's no such thing as self-esteem! How we regard, esteem, and conceptualize ourselves in relationship with God, the universe, life, and one another is central to the message of the gospel of Jesus Christ. The self of the triune model is not a selfish self but a biblical self.

Admittedly, secular pop psychology has done much to antagonize the Christian community toward this concept. We certainly are *not* to take care of ourselves in the manner that pop psychology suggests. "Looking out for number one" is translated as "sticking it to numbers two through one hundred."

Unfortunately, power partners have reacted so violently to the secularized notion of self-esteem that they have thrown the baby out with the bathwater again. The same dilemma applies to assertiveness.

The rigid mentality to understanding assertiveness is that it is license to behave in a selfish manner. When people speak up for themselves, it is considered bold, outspoken, and egotistical. However, if someone backs the car over your foot, there may be some practical validity in being bold, outspoken, and egotistical. Yet those people who feel there's no such thing as assertiveness would keep smiling in such a situation, wait for the car to eventually move, and then hand the driver a tract: ''And have a nice day!'' Right?

The Right to Say There Are No Rights?

When we, as Christians, speak of having no rights, we really mean that we subordinate our desires, intentions, feelings, and behaviors to Christ's higher will and authority. However, that doesn't mean we quit having all rights. If a member of a cult approaches us for a donation of a hundred dollars, we have the right to refuse. If we are asked to do anything ungodly that interferes with our higher duty of obedience and submission to Christ, we definitely have the right to decline. Obviously, we have rights. I would go so far as to say that we have a duty to stand up for Christ in every situation. When we don't, we sin. How we stand up for Christ, and subsequently for ourselves, is a different but associated matter. That's where assertiveness comes in. It is one tool that allows the how part to become obtainable, reachable, and potentially workable.

Right Rights

Christian assertiveness begins with implementing the Ten Commandments of Marital Respect at all times. Assertiveness must be understood across a range of interpersonal behavioral styles. This range correlates with the power-passive range of behaviors and relational styles. On one end of the continuum (see fig. 10.1) are aggressive behaviors, which correlate with the power partner, and on the opposite end are passive behaviors, which correlate with the passive partner. In the middle are assertive behaviors, which represent a balanced, respectful position for interpersonal relationships.

Aggressive	Assertive	Passive
Rigid	Christlike	Wimp
Disrespectful	Respectful	Inert
Reactive	Appropriate	Inactive
Demanding	Requesting	Yielding
Manipulative (overtly)	Nonmanipulative	Manipulative (covertly)
Controlling	Flexible	Controlled
Nonproductive	Productive	Nonproductive
An ''I count but you don't'' person	A ''you count *and* I count'' person	A ''you count but I don't'' person

Fig. 10.1. Range of behaviors.

This book is not intended to be a course in assertiveness. There are plenty of helps available—books, seminars, support groups, and classes (throughout the community)—for those who want to become assertive. I will, however, give an introduction to assertiveness because it is so potentially useful to both passive and power partners.

As figure 10.1 depicts, assertiveness is a balanced position between the power partner's aggressiveness and the passive partner's passivity. Assertiveness means an individual stands up for self in such a way as to protect personal rights or feelings while respecting the rights or feelings of the other person(s) involved. Assertive behavior conveys the message: ''You count *and* I count.'' Aggressiveness means an individual stands up for personal rights, feelings, or demands in such a way as to emotionally, relationally, or physically injure the other person(s) involved. It is self-focused and bullying. Aggressive behavior conveys the message: "I count but you don't." Passivity means an individual forfeits personal rights or feelings to keep the peace. Passive behavior conveys the message: "You count but I don't." This implied message is not spiritual servitude but psychological avoidance and self-protection.

Learning to be assertive is a skill that can be developed. A word of caution is in order, though. As with psychology in general, assertiveness should be approached from a Christian perspective. Look for authors and trainers who come from a similar orientation. The central idea is that assertiveness is one tool that can be used, in combination with the goals and methods of this book, for dewimping and derigidizing.

Using Assertiveness

Of all the peoples on this planet, Christians should be able to appreciate the usefulness of assertiveness. Assertiveness, in its broadest form, can be viewed as a timely communication that is important, warrants being heard, is clearly defined, and appreciates respect and response from its hearers and to its sender. That same working principle allowed John 3:16 to become reality.

The goals of assertiveness are to improve self-esteem; to maintain positive, healthy relationships; and to improve the likelihood that needs will be met (rather than disrespected or violated). The goal for helping the power-passive relationship is to bring both parties to a more balanced position. Assertiveness is one way of allowing such a move to middle ground by both power and passive partners from their opposite extremes. Assertiveness allows passive-dependent persons to speak up for Christ and/or themselves without injuring or threatening the other party. It allows the power person to take action that is more likely to be acceptable and to work since it takes the other party into consideration. It accomplishes the task of inclusion and consideration of both parties. The biblical message, "You count and I count, too," is communicated and experienced by both parties. It is particularly useful in handling conflict.

You count, and so does your mate.

It is a mind-set. Though there are many techniques and aspects associated with assertiveness, it is the general mentality that is so beneficial to the power-passive marriage. Of course, such a mentality is not restrained to the skilled use of assertiveness alone, but since so much has already been cultivated with this approach, its conceptual understanding and practical usefulness are helpful for power and passive partners. It also constitutes a common ground approach that can be studied, learned, and implemented in a mutual and cooperative manner.

As passive partners begin assertive behaviors, they will almost always overestimate the power of their assertiveness; they will feel they are being aggressive even when they are not yet being adequately assertive. Similarly, power partners will almost always underestimate the power of their assertiveness; they will feel they are being passive even when they are not yet being adequately assertive. The key is to base assertive self-assessment upon the mate's feedback rather than upon personal feelings in a given situation. Assertiveness support groups can also provide constructive, objective feedback. Perhaps a support group(s) can be formed to help power-passive relationships through the course of change as recommended in this book.

Assertiveness in Action

A couple of examples of assertiveness can be taken from the experiences of Lynn Lidder. The first instance is not so much a sophisticated interchange as an attitude change by Lynn that allowed her to discover she was more highly regarded by others than she regarded herself.

Lynn was unhappy with her job, but she felt she didn't deserve anything better. Obviously, she was her own worst enemy. After much soul-searching, prayer, and a little prompting, Lynn decided that she would allow herself to consider other work options. She was surprised that she quickly had several opportunities. Had she not tried, she would have perpetuated her belief that she could have nothing else.

One potential employer asked her to come for an interview some six hours away by car. Lynn anguished over how she could pull it off. She really didn't want to drive that far, and she didn't know anyone to stay with while she was there. She began feeling pessimistic and defeated before she ever left. After much arm-twisting in counseling sessions, Lynn consented to try an experiment with assertiveness. Despite her feelings, she contacted her potential employer to ask if she could receive some kind of housing assistance for her trip. Her potential boss matter-of-factly advised that the company had reserved a room in one of the city's nicest hotels for her. He also suggested that she allow the company to fly her to the interview and to fly her home early the following morning. Lynn was flabbergasted but encouraged. It had paid off to speak up for herself! The message here is that you can have an impact in relationships even if you feel that you cannot. Lynn's assertiveness prior to the interview allowed her to feel better about herself and her worth. In turn, she did well with the interview.

A second situation involved Lynn's husband, Charles. Lynn was able to integrate the Ten Commandments of Marital Respect with assertive behavior. Charles was a power partner. As Lynn began to change from her passive partner role, Charles reacted noncooperatively. Lynn recognized that, even if Charles wouldn't change, she was responsible for her life situation and for her change. She learned to show continued respect for Charles (as a person—not as a power partner) while she continued to stand up for her right to mature psychologically and spiritually.

Lynn and Charles collected antique furniture. On one occasion, Lynn could anticipate a power struggle beginning. She very much wanted a piece of furniture that perfectly matched her other pieces. For some reason, Charles decided to be belligerent about the potential purchase. Rather than exchange unpleasantries and then wimp out, Lynn began to praise Charles in front of those present for his knowledge of antique furniture. Lynn combined #2 (respect each other's worth), #5 (respect each other's abilities), and #8 (respect each other's need for affection and intimacy). She then used assertiveness: "Charles, I very much value your input. I wanted you to know how much I like this particular piece. If you don't think it's a bad buy, I'd like to go ahead and purchase it." Lynn got the piece. (No, she was not buttering him up; she was being truthful and appreciative, and she was recognizing that Charles's insecurity was showing. How do you distinguish between manipulation and legitimate assertiveness? The answer is that it depends on motivation. If Lynn was looking to minister according to the methods presented in this chapter regardless of payoff, the behavior was legitimate and not manipulation.)

How did it work? Lynn showed Charles respect and stood up assertively for what she wanted. She did so in a way that did not hurt or embarrass Charles in any way. Nor did it indicate any contentiousness. She was able to include him in the decision process while building him up at the same time. She stated her intentions and what she wished to do. It was not done for show or manipulation.

This same process—respect plus assertiveness—works in most situations. You won't always get what you want. But you are included, valued, and respected, and that makes you a winner every time!

Charles always watched "Monday Night Football." In the spirit of respect plus assertiveness, he asked Lynn, "I appreciate that you don't mind me watching football, even though you really don't care for it. I'd like to watch the game, but if there's something else you'd rather watch, I could turn back to football later.'' Charles combined #1 (respect for each other's feelings) and #6 (respect for Lynn's giving of herself) with an assertive request. Charles also practiced Ephesians 5:21: ''Submit to one another out of reverence for Christ.'' That's the correct use of submission. Lynn was so pleased to be included and to feel respected that she let Charles watch the whole game—and she stayed and watched it with him! Such actions don't mean Charles will always get his way. But they communicated something important to Lynn. There was no loser in the situation. The lesson is an important one: many times the mate is not looking to have his way so much as to feel appreciated, respected, and included.

This chapter has discussed the how-to's of necessary change. The how-to might best be thought of as how to count in a relationship. The message is clear: no matter how rigid or passive either spouse may be, real change is possible. Such tools as communicated respect and assertiveness will certainly make a positive impact on any marriage. These methods are particularly useful and appropriate for power-passive marriages. The remaining question is, Are you tough enough to make the necessary changes?

The following chapter looks at how tough a member of the power-passive relationship should get *if* one member won't cooperate at all—particularly if the partner continues to combat the desired change that the mate is trying to pursue and especially if not changing constitutes disobedience to Christ.

Chapter 11

HOW TOUGH IS TOUGH ENOUGH?

As we sat in the hospital room with my old friend Lee Atwater (who at the time was chairman of the National Republican Committee), he knew that his cancer was quite serious. He had been facing death on a daily basis. He confided that he was not ready to die. Our family had been praying for Lee and his family for a long time. We visited Lee in Washington the September before he experienced his seizure that led to the discovery of his brain tumor. He had complained to me of symptoms that seemed to go beyond expected stress effects. I urged him to get a complete medical checkup. I communicated with him several times after my visit and before his seizure. Each time he minimized my concerns for his health, promising to take better care of himself. He was an incredibly energized and busy person.

That morning in the hospital, my wife, Linda, and I prayed that God would allow us to witness to Lee and that He would show us clearly if Lee would be receptive to our spiritual testimony. Many years earlier, I had been healed of a tumor in my left ankle in a miraculous manner. I wanted to share with Lee about the God who loved him so much but not in a way that made it sound like God could be manipulated. When my pal needed me most, I wanted to give him my best.

At that point, very few people had seen Lee since his treatment began. The effects of his treatment on his physical appearance were upsetting to us. I could see that my friend was battling for his physical and spiritual life. My mind flashed back to our youth and my involvement in Lee's rhythm and blues band, The Upsetters Revue. That band and our experiences had meant a lot to all of us. I had to chuckle while attending the conferring of an honorary Ph.D. on Lee by the University of South Carolina when I read Lee's distinguished biography, which proudly started with his experience in the Upsetters. I admired him for that. I could visualize Lee's widely acclaimed and indescribable James Brown impersonation. I played trumpet, and Lee played lead guitar. Even then he was a natural leader who made it fun to be in that band. Through junior and senior high school, we practiced and played together (to the dismay of the Atwaters' neighbors as we blasted away at practice sessions in the garage). Lee later described those high-school days as innocent "Happy Days" and as being largely lost to the present high-school generation. We all cherished those times. Even when Lee attained prominence and fame, he was always gracious, kind, and available to his old pals. Everyone should have a friend as caring, committed, loyal, and fun as Lee was.

After a hugging and kissing ceremony upon entering the room, Lee shortly thereafter shared, "I've lived a good life. I've done most all the things I've wanted to do. I've helped to get some good men elected in this nation. I've made an album. But you know. . . I've neglected one important area in my life, and that's been the spiritual area. Have you anything to tell me about that?"

I asked if he had a Bible. He did. We shared our faith in some detail. Lee had many friends and was visited by many other folks who also shared their hopes for Christ's healing and their common love for Lee. Lee was completely open, vulnerable, and teachable. It was clear that the Lord had been working on Lee before we got there and He worked on him long after we left.

Several months later, we were thrilled to hear of Lee's complete commitment to Jesus Christ. Lee wanted everyone to experience what he had: salvation and a renewed, deeper appreciation for family, friends, and life. We don't need to wait until such issues become a matter of life and death. They already are a matter affecting quality of life, and as we have seen for the power-passive relationship, emotional, spiritual, and even physical death are not far behind.

Too often, we fail to comprehend the value of what we have until it is in danger of being lost. In situations where the power-passive relationship has become severe and dysfunctional, it can become difficult to fully appreciate the value, or potential value, of one's marriage. Yet the Lord's desire for us is the same as Lee's desire for us: to experience the joy of our salvation, and to experience a new or renewed appreciation and dedication to our mates, family, friends, and life. We are to be willing to make ourselves open, vulnerable, and teachable. We are to be willing to examine ourselves and to conform to Christ's will for us. Our goal is not to demand a miracle but to demonstrate obedience.

God wants you to experience joy.

Can you imagine what it might be like if some tragedy struck you, your mate, or one of your children? What would it be like if you were told that you had only one month to live? What would you want to do with that time? Which relationships would be most important? Would you seek Christ with a renewed zeal and depth of reality? Could you appreciate the value of what He has given you in your relationships with your family and spouse? Would you be able to put away unimportant things and feelings, and concentrate on love for Christ, mate, and family? If you would, why not start now? In a very real sense, members of a power-passive marriage are facing just such a crisis. It is already affecting quality of life. Emotional, spiritual, or even physical death are not far behind.

Getting Started Without Getting Burned

One major hurdle to overcome is that if one member of the power-passive dyad changes, the other member will also be immediately affected. One member may be able to change, and the other may not—at least not right away and possibly never. The positive way of looking at this same issue is that it takes only one person to change the entire relationship. If either the power partner or the passive partner changes the role in the relationship, the mate's role will also consequently change. Such change, however, is not necessarily greeted with open arms. Expect and anticipate resistance to change even when both parties volitionally state their best intentions to effect the needed change. Remember the damaging chains of codependency. However, perseverance, determination, consistency, and patience will bring about critical change over time.

In deciding how tough is tough enough, ask yourself, How tough am I willing to be with myself? There must be a willingness to reshape and to redefine the relationship, and to change your particular contributions, personally and relationally, to the dysfunctional system. This personal choice must be decided and maintained, regardless of your mate's decision or ongoing cooperation. This key hurdle is recognizing and owning power or passive characteristics. You must consider whether you are rigid or passive-dependent with your mate, family, Christian brother or sister, church, and/or coworker. You must be honest in examining yourself even at times when such examination may be uncomfortable or painful. "Examine and test and evaluate your own selves, to see whether you are holding to your faith and showing the proper fruits of it" (2 Cor. 13:5 AMPLIFIED).

Perseverance Without Self-Sabotage

A woman told me in all honesty, "I don't think that I can make the changes. They will upset my husband too much." Her comments serve as an example of the passive-dependent's distorted perception. The dear woman was basically saying, in disguised form, "He counts. I don't count." Even after understanding the way she treated herself, and after comprehending what she needed to do, she fell back into her old way of thinking and behaving. Her husband wasn't even around. She did it entirely to herself. Her husband was almost incidental to her faulty cognitions and perceptions. Leaving him, therefore, was *not* the key to getting better. She needed to concentrate on herself. She would only re-create similar problems in another relationship if she left her husband. Leaving her husband wouldn't change anything. It would only bring in another player in the same game. Instead, she needed to take responsibility for understanding herself, for learning to cope effectively with her present life situation, and for following Christ and the triune model of living.

The healthier each member is psychologically, the better the likelihood of real change. The more dysfunctional each member is, the worse the prognosis. If the power-passive dynamic is a relational problem alone, the prognosis is good. If the power-passive dynamic is a deeper, ingrained personality problem for one or both members, the prognosis is more guarded. Allowing the relationship to remain the same won't work either because it's dysfunctional already. Such dysfunctional relationships don't get better on their own. They always get worse.

The Weapon of the Wimp

The passive partner fights dirty. The passive partner is not always surrendering, discouraged, or depressed. The passive partner can become angry but is not direct with the anger. The passive partner is capable of storing up intense, prolonged anger and resentment. When the anger is turned inwardly, symptoms like depression and discouragement appear. When it is directed outwardly, it becomes an instrument of combat. The weapon of the passive partner is called passive-aggressiveness. Passive-aggressiveness can be thought of as firing the gun without emitting sound or smoke. It is disguised, indirect expression of hostility, and it is perhaps more maddening than open, direct anger.

Passive-aggressiveness includes the silent treatment, withdrawal, and manipulative behavior designed to anger the other party. The silent treatment occurs when the passive partner decides not to speak at all. A variation involves speaking only in a distant, superficial manner. Withdrawal occurs when the passive partner establishes physical and/or emotional distance: wanting to be alone, no longer performing household duties, staying away from the mate, especially sexually, or responding in a matter-of-fact way. Manipulative behavior includes dawdling and being late when the power partner is frustrated by tardiness.

The inability to tolerate expressions of anger and disapproval, and the fear of being rejected, can push passive partners into indirect ways of expressing feelings. They may say yes, but sabotage whatever plans are available. This pattern of behavior was brought home to me by a couple who sought counseling for a marital problem. It took only one session to reveal that they fit the power-passive description. The wife would retaliate her pain at being controlled by cleaning the toilet with her husband's toothbrush. That fact came out during a joint session, and her husband's aghast response could probably have been heard a mile away.

Another woman told me that her power husband demanded she keep a perfectly clean house. He ordered her to have all of the trash carried to the front of their driveway on the day the garbage truck arrived. There was absolutely no way she was going to let him order her around like that. Though she wouldn't stand up directly to him. she busied herself with so many other household chores that she didn't get the trash emptied. After much hurried yelling and complaining, the power husband ended up carrying the trash out to catch the garbage truck coming down the street. The passive wife was still smiling as she told me how upset that made her husband and how she secretly laughed as he had to do the very task he thought he could order her to do!

Other women or men fantasize or engage in extramarital affairs as a way of expressing passive-aggressive anger. Of course, this behavior is grossly unbiblical. Yet passive partners, looking the other way or rationalizing their needs, still do it. It is an extreme and desperate response to an extreme and despairing situation.

A husband who is the passive partner may be late for meals at home because he is playing golf to demonstrate that he is not controlled by any household schedule. He may also perform his chores in a passive way, letting things worsen or go undone as a show of his importance or control.

Passive-aggressive behavior won't help the situation. Though it may feel good to the passive partner, it only adds fuel to the fire. Passive-aggressiveness is a weapon that backfires, and the relationship becomes wounded. Christ can never honor rebellion or disobedience. (The power partner is also quite capable of engaging in passive-aggressive behavior, even though it is usually more skillfully implemented by, and is under the rightful domain of, the passive partner. A power partner who doesn't already know how to use passive-aggressive behaviors learns fast.)

A Mistake in the First Place

A related type of anger occurs when the passive-dependent spouse has been so angry for so long that the person rationalizes, ''I never really loved my mate in the first place. It was a mistake that we ever married at all. We are incompatible. I see it clearly now.'' This statement is a prelude to thinking about divorce. It paves the way for getting out of the relationship. It is dangerous. It is incorrect. Perceptions usually become distorted in codependent relationships. There is no need to act impulsively or impetuously.

Bringing out the worst in each other does not mean being incompatible. It simply means that the levels of anger have reached boiling-over levels. The passive-aggressive spouse must also be aware of a possible backlash of stored-up anger. Such anger needs to be dealt with appropriately to get back on track relationally. Incompatibility talk usually means repressed anger and hopelessness of resolution. But things are *not* hopeless. The idea is to think in terms of ending the negative aspects of the relationship, not the entire relationship, ending the old codependent, power-passive relationship and establishing a new Christ-dependent life; and growing in Christ as the necessary steps are undertaken to change individually and then relationally.

Even after they realize their passivity and the subsequent need for assertiveness, most passive partners continue to fear speaking up. Often, passive partners cringingly await retaliation or abusive reaction as they begin to be assertive with power partners. Passive partners can use the potency of the anger's energy in a constructive fashion by allowing it to push their attempts at assertiveness. This energy can motivate them to move ahead with becoming the persons that Christ wants them to be for Him, in marriage, and for themselves. They must be careful in the anger not to be aggressive when they think they are being assertive.

They must also remember that there will be many times when they feel that the behavior is aggressive but they behave only marginally assertive. Again, we come back to the importance of the principle of balance. I recommend assertiveness classes so that feedback from instructors and peers can be given as assertiveness is learned, rehearsed, and implemented (in class and at home).

Warning About Anger

At the beginning of this book, there was a warning that reading the material contained here can prove hazardous to one's psychological health. There is a natural tendency to become destructively angry and resentful. This happens as the passive partner increasingly realizes just what has been going on in the relationship in a more focused manner. This happens as the power partner is made to feel criminally exposed and discovers that the former way of relating to the mate is no longer satisfactory.

Both parties need to channel this energy into a response to godly living rather than target each other. Both parties have played a key part in establishing and maintaining the dysfunctional, codependent existence. Such an arrangement has served each member equally well. The love exerted in bearing each other's anger and burdens will be multiplied and returned a hundredfold. It will take some time to relearn, readjust, and implement the information presented in this book. As the relational healing progresses, deep and meaningful appreciation and love develop concurrently—and are primed to last a lifetime! (See also 1 Cor. 13.)

The Challenge of Godliness

This book, though directed at the power-passive dynamic, is legitimately nothing less than a call to holiness. If you and your mate are believers, you share common ground in your quest to follow Christ. It's not so easy to spot or overcome the psychological impediments that prevent personal growth and relational health. Just as Adam was incomplete without Eve (and vice versa) spouses not working together are functionally incomplete. You and your mate need each other. That is why God brought you together in the first place.

My prayer is that both members in the relationship will always remember the covenant with God concerning the marital vows. If each or preferably both will seek after Christ in the spirit of that covenant, He will honor that commitment and heal your relationship. Your marital covenant included your mate *and* Christ. It was a three-way commitment. Even at times when you are tempted to forget your part, Christ will not forget His part. Second Timothy 2:13 reminds us that "if we are faithless, He remains faithful; for He cannot deny Himself" (NASB). Challenge and encourage each other with this truth.

Encourage your mate.

Each can take on the role and function of the other in collateral relationships. Each member is trying to move toward the middle of the power-passive continuum to achieve, and then to maintain, balance. The power partner is not the true opposite of the passive-dependent counterpart, though there are certain behaviors of each that are. Moving toward the middle feels unnatural and alien for each. Such movement may frighten individuals into feeling that they may have gone too far. But that's hardly ever the case.

Accountability

Accountability is always in order, especially when the power-passive dynamic has been recognized. In all honesty, who can really complain about going to a respected authority to ascertain if your marriage is on track? Certainly, you don't want to go to a rigid leader. Both members should agree on whom to see. This kind of help legitimately comes under church discipline. Church discipline can be retributive and advisory. There need not be any power-passive family secrets. Find a trusted helper and lay out all the issues.

When seeking accountability and support, let your mate save face and let your mate wholly face the self. Don't throw a pie in the face. Don't wimp out. You are rejecting your mate's, and your own, dysfunctional role—not your mate's, or your own, position in the relationship as delegated by Christ.

Be willing to give your mate the benefit of the doubt at times when intentions seem injurious. Check out all your assumptions, and never assume what your mate meant. Remember that your perceptions have become colored by your negative past experiences. Try to put the past behind you and work on repairing the relationship in the present. Try to encourage your mate, despite your unpleasant feelings, rather than criticize, blame, or ventilate negative feelings or thoughts.

Beware of the Discouragers

Some parties are attended by poopers, and some churches are attended by discouragers. These folks stand on the sidelines and interfere with good things that are happening. Don't let others discourage, condemn, or make you feel guilty about what you are doing to change. Don't expect everyone to understand. Some people will want you "fixed" because you scare them. You may be confronting them with the fact that life may be more difficult, or complicated, than they had anticipated. You may be scaring other passive partners that they need to take action. You may be threatening other power partners that they need to change. Similarly, don't let your spouse push you, or slow you, in your individual growth process.

If there is continued resistance to change by either member, seek help without procrastination. You don't need that other member's presence to make needed changes, though it definitely helps. If there are other complicating factors (e.g., substance abuse, being an adult child of a dysfunctional family, other emotional or personal problems), don't hesitate to seek appropriate professional counseling.

What About Divorce or Separation?

If the power-passive couple has begun working on issues mentioned in the previous chapters (e.g., learning to communicate more effectively, increasing relational intimacy, learning and practicing biblical assertiveness, refusing to play power-passive games, observing the Ten Commandments of Marital Respect), that couple has already taken tremendous steps in overcoming the power-passive dysfunction. However, some individuals reading this book are ready to get out of the marriage. There are no biblical grounds for divorce on the basis of rigidity or passivity alone.

At times of stress such as may have occurred in the power-passive relationship, individuals develop tunnel vision. The ability to see things clearly becomes obscured and narrowed. The passive partner becomes rigid, and the power partner becomes more rigid. The world and emotional options are viewed as if looking through blinders. Now is not the time to invest in the stock market. Now is not the time to make major decisions about anything—especially about ending the marriage.

At such pressure points, it is very difficult, if not impossible, to see any way a particular marriage has any hope of making it. Yet miracles do happen. Change can still happen. But what if one's mate still fights and refuses to cooperate? What can be done if one's mate continues to do obvious things designed to demonstrate resistance and noncooperation? If God hates divorce, is it ever permissible to separate? If so, is there ever a time to consider separation?

Separation is a somewhat controversial area. Just as there are well-meaning ministers and counselors who may advise divorce, there are folks who may prematurely push separation. There are also times when couples come for counseling with the predetermined mind-set of separation. First Corinthians 7:10–11 advises against separation: "To the married I give this command (not I, but the Lord): A wife must not separate from her husband. But if she does, she must remain unmarried or else be reconciled to her husband. And a husband must not divorce his wife.'' Throughout Scripture, the ideas of separation and divorce are connected. They are not two different processes as in modern-day understanding. In biblical usage, these terms are aspects of the same operation.

It is beyond the purview of this book to examine in detail this passage in relationship to the larger teachings on divorce and marriage found throughout Scripture. However, it seems clear that God is against divorce (though I believe there are legitimate loopholes, i.e., sexual sin *[porneia]*, which includes adultery *[moichao]*, and desertion by a nonbelieving mate). Scripture teaches that God is strongly promarriage and profamily (see Jer. 3; Matt. 5:32; 19:4–9; 1 Cor. 7:10–15). Therefore, it seems that the higher principle is the preservation, dignity, and sanctity of marriage.

If separation, in the modern sense, is done at all, it should be done after much prayerful deliberating and after obtaining wise counsel. Scripture seems to recognize that separation is permissible if it is done as a last resort to avoid divorce and if it is done with the aim of reconciliation as its end product. In this manner separation is used as the means of securing the higher principle of the preservation and sanctity of marriage.

It also seems that the personal and relational dignity of the marriage is of primary importance in maintaining hope for the preservation and sanctity of marriage. Unfortunately, in today's fallen world, there are blatant, as well as insidious, threats to marital dignity. Though this is a personal judgment, I do recommend separation, with this above understanding, especially in counseling situations where there are threats of violence, danger, or irreparable harm to the dignity of the marriage.

Sometimes separation is unavoidable. Sometimes it is necessary to break through the power partner's denial that the mate could really choose to live without the power partner and actually do it. Sometimes it is necessary to prove to the passive partner that the individual really can do things previously felt to be insurmountable.

Separation should never be done impulsively, defiantly, or manipulatively. Such things aren't so readily discernible to either spouse, especially due to psychological defense mechanisms that also distort a spouse's views. Separation should be seen as a cooling off period for the purpose of refueling in order to avoid further harm, pain, or escalation of conflict, which may threaten the very fabric of the marital relationship. The word *refueling* highlights the idea of a return trip home. *Refueling* may include working through feelings, repentance, and forgiveness. If counseling has not already been obtained, it most certainly is appropriate at this juncture.

Should separation occur, marital partners cannot rest or feel that it is time-out with no consequences about which to be concerned. The clock keeps ticking. With every passing day it becomes that much harder to get back together. Time is not always a healer. Many times it is a silent killer! When a race car makes a pit stop, the pit crew quickly and diligently services the vehicle. Should the driver sit back, kick off his shoes, and chow down on a piece of pie without concern for getting back in the race, the rest period would assuredly cost that driver, and the crew, the race. Similarly, being separated and refueling should not be confused with kicking back and dropping out of the race. Now is the time to work hard on repairing the dignity of the relationship to effect reconciliation.

Separation is a crisis time. The Lord is near and willing to help the wounded through crises. He desires to work healing, restoration, and holiness in your life as you lean on Him. Be encouraged of this promise: there is victory in Christ! Once reconciliation has been attained, it is time to immediately get back on track with the directives of this book.

Chapters 6 through 11 have outlined specific tasks involved in defeating characterological and/or relational rigidity and passive-dependency. The suggestions will have a very real impact on the dysfunctional, codependent dynamic. Real change and Christian growth are available despite any apparent obstruction. Christ continues to be in the healing and creating business.

Chapter 12

SPIRITUAL THREATS TO THE POWER-PASSIVE MARRIAGE

It was against my better judgment, but I decided to let my son, Peter, have his buddy, Griffy, sit with us at church. Boys will be boys, and those two were very definitely boys that were boys when they got together. They weren't bad at all. In fact, they were fun. But at that age (at that time, Peter was ten and still smaller than I), they sometimes had a hard time stopping their fun and could become silly at times when others around us were trying to focus on the worship service. Peter never quite understood how I knew about such things, and he assumed I was born in my thirties wearing wing tips and lecturing on the virtues of a clean bedroom.

On this particular Sunday, we had the pleasure of taking my grandmother with us. Nanna sat at the end of the pew, to my far right, with Griffy next to her and Peter between Griffy and me. Peter recognized my stern father look that I shot off at him during several parts of the service, signaling, "I'm watching you guys so you had better be on your best behavior!" My stern look usually worked pretty well, and Peter would sit up straight while his pupils dilated the instant he saw it—even if he was already sitting up straight with his pupils dilated. It was a conditioned response.

When my seat started jiggling, I became suspicious. As I glanced quickly at Peter, his posture was straight and his face solemn, but upon closer scrutiny, I could see that his body was twitching. Griffy was the same way, but when they glanced at each other, little bursts of air snorted out their noses. Their bodies began to vibrate the entire pew. Their hands went simultaneously across their mouths in a crude attempt to muffle a giggle, which only created a louder gulping sound with half snorts. I fired off a ferocious stern father look to no avail. Their shoulders drew up, and their free hands were clasped to their sides while a second round of choked grunts attempted to hide deep belly laughs stuck sideways in their throats.

I did exactly what any loving father would have done when his stern father look failed: I reached over and placed my hand onto Peter's trapezius muscle in an attempt to apply a Mr. Spock grip. I missed and somehow struck a ticklish area. (My son has always been ticklish all over his entire body—even his hair.) He surely reasoned that because Dad had tickled him it was permissible to laugh. I could plainly hear what sounded like the beginning of an eruption of a nasaled guffaw when I leaned over and whispered a stern father command, "PETER! STOP IT!" He sat up straight, eyes bugged out, and tried to speak to me. But I wouldn't let him. I authoritatively told him that he was on restriction. As I was further clarifying his restriction, he interrupted, "But, Dad . . ." I said, "Don't interrupt me when I'm disciplining you." He pointed to Nanna. I discovered that she had dozed off and fallen onto Griffy, who was totally taken aback and embarrassed. She had begun to make little guttural sounds as she exhaled and nodded on Griffy's shoulder.

I then noticed that the people in the pew behind us had been observing the entire episode. Their pew was quivering, and several were squeezing their noses as they leaned over with their arms across their stomachs. No longer able to restrain herself, one party let out a polite but abrupt cough, thereby jolting Nanna into an upright posture with a nod of her head as if to demonstrate her approval of the pastor's point. I had overreacted, based on partial information, and had been too quick to judge Peter. I wasn't aware that I lacked the complete information necessary to make an appropriate judgment about Peter's behavior. In the very same way, there will be well-meaning people at church, at work, and even at home who may make premature judgments based on incomplete information about what they see and understand of power-passive processes. A shell-shocked passive partner may well be wounded by the very people sought out for relief, comfort, and assistance.

Even when loved ones, church friends, or Christian leaders disappoint or frustrate you because they don't understand (due to various forms of deception), you must remember the quiet Partner who is not passive but actively shares your sadness, grief, and marital covenant. He will bear you up. Lean on Him.

Remember also that there is another, with many followers, who is cheering on your demise and raising the banner of disorder, discouragement, and defeat on your behalf. Satan is quite real, and the evil in the world is more evil and pervasive than we want to believe. He sows confusion, delusion, disillusion, disunity, deception, and rigidity and reaps impotent believers so wounded with their personal battles that they lose their salt and light in the world and forfeit their victory in Christ over the Enemy's attacks. Power-passivity in relationships and in the church is a subtle but effective weapon that knocks the legs right out from under the person(s) attired in Christian battle fatigues.

Spiritual Warfare

Several years ago on an airplane trip, a pastor noticed a man who had refused the flight attendant's offer of a lunch tray. The man explained that he was fasting. The pastor approached him, anticipating spiritual fellowship, only to discover that the man was a follower of Satan. As many other followers had agreed to do, he was fasting and praying for the demise of Christian marriages across the land!

There is spiritual warfare in the heavenly realm. I am more convinced than ever of the pervasive reality of spiritual warfare, and a primary target of the Enemy is the Christian marriage. The power-passive life-style does not serve God's interests (see Eph. 6:12). It is a perversion of biblical love and marriage. In the Christian community, rigidity is just as destructive as it is in marital relationships. It often goes unrecognized, but its effects are most definitely felt. Various forms of rigidity operate the same way as rigidity does in Christian marriages. But in the church, rigidity can appear correct.

The church is not only a hospital for sinners but also an intensive care unit for emotionally wounded marriages. The ability to experience and enjoy healthy relationships—individually and maritally beyond the limitations of the power-passive dyad—is essential for spiritual and psychological growth. Just as Christian fellowship is vital for individual Christian growth, Christian fellowship is vital for healthy marital development and sustenance and/or marital healing and restoration.

Marital healing must be aggressively available from the church. Unfortunately, due to lack of information, misinformation, and power-passive processes in the church, destructive relationships sometimes go unnoticed, and cries for help fall on deaf ears.

Throughout the ages, most spiritual arguments have pitted the church against secular society. I believe that one of Satan's means of attack for this decade centers on infighting within the church. Rigidity is one such form of infighting. Just as individual and marital rigidity subtly attacks and destroys the family and individual members of the family, corporate rigidity splits and attacks the members of the body of Christ. Our unity and oneness in Christ are polarized. We are maneuvered into positions of attacking one another in the name of purity, holiness, and encouragement. Instead of learning to work together toward purity, ethical and moral behavior, and godliness, we may instead defend our rigid positions, which are unconsciously based on psychological needs rather than on biblical instruction.

Discipline, perseverance, and obedience, based on correct spiritual mandates, are always right. Rigidity, passivity, and insistence, based on incorrect psychological needs, are always wrong.

No Easy Answers

The guest preacher had nearly completed a series on what he termed *encouragement*. He tried earnestly to encourage his audience, yet he actually discouraged more than a few. He argued that all a hurting believer needed to do was to turn problems over to Christ. He presented many references concerning the concept. Who could argue with such a plain truth? The preacher stated it was selfish to think of yourself. It was ''secular'' to put yourself first. He argued that self-esteem was invalid for Christians because Christians were always to put others first. I afterward discovered that many hurting people in that service felt worse. They felt selfish for tending to their wounds. They felt inadequate, guilty, disobedient, and discouraged because they couldn't seem to turn their problems over to Christ, even though they wanted to do just that. The preacher had no understanding of the identified self of the triune model.

One woman later confided that such a message angered her. She had just begun to understand that her burnout and depression had come from putting others first too much of the time while neglecting herself. (That, incidentally, is why burnout occurs—God did not intend for us to neglect ourselves. There must be balance.) The preacher admonished her that the solution to her problems was more of the same! Obviously, ''more'' was not better. She needed permission to lessen the overload, not add to it.

Another woman told me that her depression had deepened, and she didn't want to hear more of the particular series for fear she would feel even worse. The message she heard was, ''Your feelings and experiences don't count. Quit your sniveling and start acting like a *real* Christian should!'' Yet her feelings and experiences were valid and legitimate. She desperately needed to hear that Christians have struggles, too. She needed to know that she is of inestimable worth and personally counts to Christ, and that she counts in her church. But she didn't have ears to hear—not because of her spiritual ability but because of her psychological inability. She needed to know how to turn her problems over to Christ. That sermon made her feel like a failure again.

She needed to know how to take her eyes off her sin and look to Christ. She wanted to know how to see the sufficiency of Christ when she was rendered insufficient to see Him herself. She needed to be guided in love to the Savior and to His attributes and promises rather than abandoned to try to find Him in her emotionally battered state.

Unconditional love makes healing possible.

She needed permission to share her pain and work through her feelings and problems with someone who could help her find Christ's healing. She needed support to determine if there were unidentified spiritual or psychological barriers that blocked her pathway to Christ's healing. She wanted freedom to seek and to receive such help rather than to feel inadequate or guilty about having to do it all by herself when she couldn't. She needed unconditional love from her fellow Christians rather than rejection for not being a good enough believer. She needed to be loved for who she was regardless of where she was emotionally. Such love would, in turn, set the stage for emotional growth and healing. She needed loving support and acceptance while she faced the pain of her power-passive existence: "Bear one another's burdens, and thus fulfill the law of Christ" (Gal. 6:2 NASB).

This situation is not an isolated one by any means. This same message is repeated in many churches. The power partner mind-set dictates that things are either right or wrong, and that individuals should be able to right their wrongs instantly, thereby receiving blessings and victorious living. But it doesn't work that way. When sin is identified, the obvious first line of attack is to stop the sinful behavior. But there are also other times when things aren't so easy.

Over the course of my training as a psychologist, I remember many occasions when well-meaning Christians learned this lesson the hard way. Newcomers to the psychiatric unit would go to patients' rooms and pray and use scriptural admonishments. They would try everything they could think of at least twice and then leave the unit feeling frustrated, confused, and discouraged. They expected genuine change and quick results, but they got none. They utilized every kind of spiritual approach they knew of with the patients but to no avail. There are no easy answers.

Does that mean spiritual approaches and psychological problems don't mesh? Not at all. But rigid approaches don't work any better here than they do in power-passive relationships. They may look right, but they don't work. They may feel right, but they don't really help.

One common misconception concerning depression will serve as an example of what I mean. Power partners believe that individuals suffering from any form of depression have the ability, by faith or obedience, to pick themselves up from the depths of depression and get back on the right spiritual track. That isn't true. Though some milder forms of depression could respond to biblical admonishment and directives alone, there are definitely forms of depression where individuals are incapable of picking themselves up at all without proper professional help. Many times, such individuals cannot connect to God at all much less follow well-meaning directives that essentially say to "shape up" or to "trust God" or to "turn the matter over to God." Such "help" isn't help. It only aggravates the condition.

Another common misconception held by power partners is that there aren't such psychological things as unconscious processes. Such things are dismissed as being satanic, nonexistent, or immaterial. Yet the truth is that such psychological processes may play a major part in many psychological or spiritual problems. This book has demonstrated how the power-passive dynamic operates, yet neither personality is fully aware of all that is going on. Many parts and features of this co-dependent relationship happen at an unconscious level. Another related premise is that Christian communities can be rigid and participate in unconscious activities on a larger, communal scale that function similarly to the dynamics of the power-passive relationship.

The triune model of humankind has definite implications for understanding human beings and helping them when they encounter problems. To do so competently, the helper must have at least a basic understanding of theology (relationship with God); a basic understanding of psychology (understanding self); and a basic understanding of relationships, systems, and psychodynamics (relationship with others). The more training and experience in each area, the more constructive the real understanding is, and the more effective the helper is.

Our offices get phone calls from prospective clients wanting to check us out in advance of coming in for help. Many times the question is posed, ''What approach do you use?'' I have to reply, ''Approach to what?'' The typical response is, ''To counseling.'' I have to educate callers that their inquiry is a lot like phoning a physician and asking the physician to guess what's wrong with them without any examination or further information. I also tell such callers that there is no single approach for all of the varying degrees and dimensions of psychological problems.

The more instruments and medication the physician takes in the bag on a house call, the more likely the physician will have something that will be useful for treatment. Just prescribing penicillin in a shotgun approach doesn't work in every situation. Similarly, the more tools a counselor has in the bag, the more likely the counselor will have something that will be useful for treatment. We wouldn't feel very confident in flying with a pilot who had only a "crash" course in piloting! And if I'm having a heart attack, I want to go to the facility with all the best equipment, the most highly trained doctors, and the finest reputation.

When it comes to many forms of psychological understanding, power partners are impatient, close-minded, extremes-oriented, legalistic, and authoritative. They have to resist psychological perspectives not because of their validity but because of the implications and ramifications that such a point of view affords. They become potentially exposed; they feel apprehensively threatened; they react defensively; they resist understanding and change. In their resistance, a false feeling of control permeates their receptivity.

Many well-meaning Christians don't understand psychological or personal problems, but they think they do. Often, their understanding is naive, oversimplified, misinformed, short-sighted, or unrealistic. They unknowingly try to pigeonhole problems for their convenience, or for what they think is the right thing to do, rather than for truth or legitimate assistance. For some Christians, there must be black-and-white solutions to life's stresses. For power partners, problems cannot be complex, varied, time-consuming, or unclear. There must be a quick, clearly defined plan of action available. If they can't come up with such a plan, they will naturally turn to others who have developed shallow strategies for coping with the pressures of life. Then they can feel that all is well and there is an easy answer for every problem that comes their way. This feeling is reinforced when uncomplicated problems are resolved through one-two-three step mechanisms.

Problems of daily living do respond to scriptural confrontation, clarification, and/or accountability. Scripture, however, is not so much a cookbook of simple recipes for every life problem as a trustworthy compass to healing truth. In some of life's tougher situations, especially in complex psychological or relational difficulties, it is wise to have someone help you who may be more knowledgeable about the use of a compass plus things like wind factors, tide, charting, and navigational procedures.

I remember working with my first MPD (multiple personality disorder) on an early internship. I had studied about MPD but had never experienced one. I had picked up on the fact that our patient was MPD when it was not yet officially diagnosed. My supervisor told me there was no such thing in this case, and even if there was, it wasn't pertinent to the handling of the particular case. The supervisor met with the patient that day and released her to go home because she told him everything seemed to be going okay. On her way out, I asked to speak with her. I discovered that a second personality, within the same patient, was waiting for the patient to leave the premises to bodily take over. Had the unconscious not been considered, the patient would be dead because the second personality had planned suicide. My supervisor didn't believe there was MPD, so he didn't follow up sufficiently. Simply believing something isn't true, or not understanding it, doesn't make it untrue. Yet that is exactly the way the power partner operates.

Power partners don't understand deeper psychological processes such as personality disorders, either. Individuals with personality disorders have very real disadvantages that are discounted or dismissed by the power partner community. Many clients have reported feeling demoralized, discouraged, frustrated, and abandoned by power people who could not understand them and placed expectations that were too high on them. One rather mature Christian told me she felt angry when, at a Christian conference for hurting people, the leaders expected her to be able to perform faster than she could. She noticed another individual starting to psychologically decompensate (the process of literally falling apart emotionally) under the same pressure. There was no apparent understanding of the psychological process going on with the observed party, and no psychological help necessary for her to move forward therapeutically. The push made her feel hurried, discounted, inadequate, guilty, and resentful.

Other clients have reported attending Christian seminars where information was disseminated that caused them, and many others, to experience considerable psychological distress without any attention given to their ignited emotional turmoil. Another client told me such "helpers must not have had any real problems of their own—only situations that they thought were tough. They don't seem to be able to connect or to understand a certain level of distress. I sometimes wish that such people could experience real pain and what I feel, so they could begin to understand. Then I feel guilty for having such thoughts."

The rigid mentality assumes that individuals are either hurting emotionally or not hurting at all. They don't understand that there is a therapeutic progression and a timely graduation from numerous stages of pain depending on the extent of that particular pain; the psychological resources and dimensions of individual capability; the knowledge, training, and effectiveness of the helping agent; the availability of support systems; social-environmental influences; and spiritual resources and levels of development.

In psychology, timing and personal readiness are significant. In theology, the process of revelation also required timing and personal readiness. God didn't give us everything at once. Yet in our "gimme, gimme" world, we want things fast and complete. We sometimes place higher demands on other Christians for a particular area than God places on us for that same area.

Many things don't fit neatly into the power partner's mold of the world. Psychology is one of them. Psychological processes and understanding are threatening to the controller life-style of the power partner, who fears exposure and loss of control. Subsequently, the power partner denies, undermines, sabotages, and minimizes their psychological legitimacy. The partner can do so individually, familially, or corporately through the local church or parachurch organizations.

There are no easy answers or quick fixes. McDonald's will never go into the counseling business, and Christian psychologists will never have drive-through windows. If they do, drive right on by! It's not an either-or situation. There is room for theology and psychology. One is not wrong, and the other is right. Both are part of God's revelation and can enhance and supplement each other. They must be biblically integrated and balanced. Both must be filtered through Scripture. Theology comes first and teaches us how to study God. Psychology comes next and teaches us how to understand ourselves, particularly in relationship with God, and how we can filter theology through psychology.

We need theology and psychology.

We are quite capable of interpreting Scripture and theology in a tainted manner because of our sin nature and because of our psychological neediness. Psychology must always be aligned with theology. When drugs are prescribed by competent, caring physicians, drugs are good and useful. These same drugs, used on the streets, become bad and harmful. It's not the drugs per se but how they are used. The same applies to psychology. It's not psychology per se but how it is used. If screened through Scripture, aligned with theology, and employed by competent, caring, reputable helpers who are followers of Christ, psychology has much to offer to the Christian community. Ignoring, fearing, minimizing, or resisting psychology can be equally dangerous to the functioning of present-day Christianity: its leaders, its people, its life-style, and its impact.

We Are Not Created Equal

It is a myth to think that all people are equal. We're not even created equal. Some of us come with the genetic potential to be geniuses; some come with the genetic potential to be schizophrenic; some are affected by parents who are abusive in various ways; some are affected by physical disease or impairment; some are affected by psychological impairment. We are different. We are unique. Though we may become one in Christ, and though we may be born again, we maintain vestiges of our uniqueness. Though we have much in common, share similar life struggles, and fight against the flesh and the same satanic forces, we remain unique.

A misperception by the power-passive community is that we are all the same—what works for me will work for you. Such perceptions give a feeling that the world is predictable and that power persons can control, at least to some extent, what happens in this otherwise unsafe planet. Rigid mentalities find it difficult to grasp the concept that we can be the same and different at the same time. They see their mates' differentness as threatening rather than as complementing their abilities. Similarly, other members of the body of Christ, who may see things differently from the way they do, are considered somehow adversarial.

Overprotection of the Church

This same guardedness can become overprotection. We are to be in the world but not of it (see Matt. 5:14; Rom. 12:2; 1 John 2:15–17). The power partner must be careful not to put trust in ritual rather than in the living God. A delicate balance must be maintained. The power partner must be open to learning additional ways to grow spiritually, psychologically, and relationally yet not be open to false teaching. Similarly, the church must protect its own while developing them in these same areas. It must not overreact, but it dare not underreact, either. There are tension and balance to practical Christian living.

A Closed System

Communal rigidity can lead to a closed system mentality. We become too comfortable with convenience. We close ourselves off. We become stagnant. We resist new relationships or changes in routine. We appreciate our Christian friendships, but we don't cultivate non-Christian friendships. We withdraw from the world. We neglect evangelization. We can sit and talk about the virtues of missions, but we don't go out and evangelize. We become comfortable without growth and without evangelization. We fail to act on the Great Commission, aborting our purpose of penetrating society for Christ. Communal rigidity affects the church the same way codependent rigidity affects a marriage: it appears that all is well when injury is occurring that can lead to death.

Legalism in the Church

Communal rigidity can also lead to legalism in the church. The mind-set is that there is only one way to do things. Things must absolutely go by the book, but that book is not necessarily the Bible. Rules and structure come first. Christ comes next. People come last. A variation of this rigidity occurs when we twist the Bible to strictly enforce a view we hold rather than form our view in compliance with the directives of the Bible.

A related form of legalism is that only certain people know what's best for the church, so everyone else must conform to their authority. Another form of legalism is the extremes-oriented mind-set dictating that things are either all right or all wrong. With biblical truths, that's right, but with gray areas and nonspecifics, that's not necessarily right. Trying new hymns or worship experiences during a service, for example, may not be too popular in a ritualistic or formalized ceremony, but it is not necessarily wrong, either. Creativity of worship does not have to compete with traditional worship for rightness. Both may be appropriate, and depending on the occasion and the participants, either could be inappropriate. Not everything needs to be characterized as all right or all wrong.

Legalism reduces Christianity to a religion. It robs Christians of experiencing a vibrant relationship with Jesus Christ. Religion cannot save us—only Christ can do that. One of the main things that distinguishes genuine Christianity from other world religions is having a personal relationship with the object of the religion. All religions offer practice, but only Christianity offers more than practice and ritual. Legalism produces self-righteousness, hypocrisy, and ultimate spiritual immaturity or stagnation.

Time Bombs

Because of power partners' need for structure, they let activities, functions, and events order their world rather than order their world and then work in prioritized activities. In our high-tech society, we have sacrificed time to accommodate activity. There are so many things going on that we dare not miss a single one of them! Again, it's a matter of balance. There's nothing wrong with involvement unless it prevents other, more important involvement. If we're so busy taking ourselves or our kids to so many events or activities that we neglect quality family time and spiritual development, we had better take another look at what's really being gained.

The Negative Impact of Rigid Leadership

Rigid leaders must be careful to control their psychological need to control. Rigid leaders can be tempted to use their position and authority to influence and control for the wrong psychological reasons rather than serve and give as servant-leaders for the right spiritual reasons. This type of leadership is not leadership at all.

A test for rigid leadership is the allegiance factor. Rigid leaders demand allegiance and loyalty to their leadership and are not fully open to followers of Christ who may point out dissimilarities. Rigid leaders can feel betrayed if their followers are not unquestionably 100 percent behind them—even if there's one small area of question or uncertainty. They won't come right out and say it, but their attitude reflects "it's my way or no way!'' Severely rigid leaders will find ways to silence, punish, distance, or discredit dissenters.

Rigid Leadership and Dysfunction Within the Church

Rigid leaders, whether mildly rigid or severely rigid, are difficult to work with or to follow. What applies to power partners and to their effects on passive partners can also apply to rigid leaders' impact on the members of the local body of Christ. This is especially true when there are other rigid persons with their own agendas, when there are passive-dependent persons who already react negatively to rigid leadership, and when there are emotionally wounded persons who are affected in a sensitively defensive and/or exaggerated way.

For example, if some members have suffered some form of emotional, physical, or sexual abuse, the individuals will react in a heightened and exacerbated manner. Rigidity is a form of abuse. When people have already been abused, they are extremely reactive to any other type of abuse. For abused persons, their reaction to rigidity is done at a deep and disturbing level with various surface reactions. Not all people who have endured abusive treatment in their pasts are presently and consciously aware of it. These individuals are adept at repressing and suppressing such feelings for their psychological protection. Psychological reactions may not appear for many years later and can be triggered by things in their present that re-create their perception of abuse and the repressed memories, feelings, and thoughts. Some individuals with abusive histories have no earthly idea that those things are there. They may not have surfaced yet. (But they will.) Such dynamics become quite complex.

Suffice it to say that the power personality, leader, or mind-set can harm others in such a way that the power person would never imagine. Such injury can range from mild defensiveness to noncooperation to withdrawal to psychological symptoms to full-blown psychological decompensation. Such harm, or perception of harm, leads to splitting of families, body life, and broken churches. As America continues to become increasingly dysfunctional due to the breakup of the traditional family and Judeo-Christian teachings in the family, there will be a corresponding widening gap in churches with power leaders and members who may have some experience of abuse and/or dysfunction.

Following the Leader?

People will follow good leadership, but a rigid management style tries to control people and discourages and smothers growth. More than ever, the church needs biblical leadership—not leadership that is rigid. Severely rigid leaders surround themselves with rigid puppets. Such yes-women and yes-men affirm their leadership, allow their continuance of control, and cooperate to overwhelm dissenters.

Obviously, such severely rigid leaders would not be fully receptive to outside information that may jeopardize control or may threaten to expose them. Such rigid leaders play the same games with their congregations as power partners play with their spouses. For example, the Divide and Conquer Game can be used to prevent information that may lead to perceived exposure or to loss of control. Such things as professional counseling, books like this one, and true accountability are branded as taboo, unspiritual, or Christian weakness. As has been previously discussed, messages like ''just trust God'' can be (often unconsciously) designed to sabotage outside assistance that might threaten the leaders or their views. These rigid leaders are not truly open, receptive, or teachable, though they will give an appearance of being so in order to shore up their leadership image.

The sad part is that too many rigid leaders believe that what they are doing is the right thing. For such leaders, control, in the psychological sense, is more important than biblical leadership. Of course, they would never admit such a thing and probably would not be aware of it. But it would be felt in the church.

The consequence of such leadership is usually one of the following over time: the group becomes a cult; God replaces the leader if the leader won't change while the body is ready for growth; God removes His people from the power and control of the leader; God removes the leader to a receptive body if the leader is open to growth while the original body remains closed; God removes the candlestick if neither the leader nor the body will change.

Power–Passivity in the Church

It's a well-known operative that 20 percent of the people in the church do 80 percent of the work of that church. That's not new information. But what about the responsibilities of Christians to affect the world for Christ? Communal power-passivity allows us to lament our situations but not to act to do anything about them. Communal power-passivity refers to all of the processes and dynamics of the power and passive personalities and roles plus their interrelationship operating on a larger scale involving and affecting other members of the body of Christ. How can Christians, in good conscience, not do all they can to further the causes of Christ in the world while stopping Satan's work in the world? Yet many Christians don't vote; they don't speak out or become involved against such issues as pornography, abortion, the destruction of the traditional family, homosexuality, premarital sex, secularism in the schools, New Age tactics in education, satanic ritual abuse, and so on.

As a psychologist, I am frightened for the direction of Christianity in America. We are being attacked by all kinds of social, philosophical, spiritual, and political forces and agendas from without, while we simultaneously battle psychological and spiritual forces and agendas from within ourselves and from within Christianity. I am greatly concerned about the incredible destruction of the cornerstones of psychological health in America: the disallowance of morals and values based on our Judeo-Christian heritage and the functional and operational demise of the traditional family.

As I look back to the previous decade, I remember thinking that what was formerly considered neurotic had become normal and acceptable. Due to our modern technological world, things happen much faster than ever before. What used to take generations now takes relatively brief periods of time. As I look at the present, I see more familial dysfunction than ever. Familial dysfunction in one's family of origin causes all kinds of individual, marital, and nuclear family problems. We are reaping now what was sown in the previous decade. I shudder to think what is to come.

Communal power-passivity allows us, as followers of Christ, to sit back and watch as the world changes around us without getting sufficiently involved and without appropriate reaction. Dr. Francis Schaeffer proposed that what we have been willing to settle for has been the perception of personal peace and affluence. These things have become sufficient to allow us to be comfortably satisfied to inspire us to inaction and complacency. A similar process has occurred in the church via power-passive influences and processes.

The saying that "when you're up to your armpits in alligators, it's hard to remember that your original purpose was to clean up the swamp" applies to this power-passive effect. As a body of Christians, we can become so involved in the battle of feeling comfortable that we don't see the bigger picture. We can become so caught up and confused in our codependent forms of Christianity (e.g., individual, marital, communal power-passive paradigms) that we render ourselves emotionally and behaviorally disabled or impotent.

I believe that one of the biggest threats to Christianity in the United States as we approach the twenty-first century is communal power-passivity by the church, falsely and blindly tolerated in the name of Christ. We can become so caught up with the form and procedure of Christianity that best accommodate our unconscious psychological needs (individually, relationally, and corporately) that we neglect the true behavioral manifestation (as outlined throughout Scripture, especially in the book of

James) of the essence and substance of biblical Christianity. Rigidity in the church has become practical Pharisaism. *We must constantly strive never to let our ministry reflect our flawed personalities and unrecognized psychological needs rather than to accurately reflect Christ, and Christ working victoriously in our lives.*

The Unseen War Unveiled

Many people have the false notion that if they visited a psychologist's office, they would see Bob Newhart's Mr. Carlin, a wild-eyed Jack Nicholson, or the characters of the movie *The Dream Team*. It's not like that at all. Most of the people there are just like me and you. Many of them are the same people you might find on your pew at church. When they get behind the doctor's closed office door, they reveal inner, deeper, more personal struggles that would not be apparent in the waiting room. That's the way it is with the power-passive dynamic. It affects individual lives, marriages, and families, and it infiltrates the church in a way that is not so much readily detectable as it is emotionally and spiritually felt.

The purpose of this book has been to bring the power-passive dynamic out of the waiting room and into the doctor's office. It is my hope that the dynamics have been brought into the light and into a more focused position so that help and healing can be effected. The process has begun. It's now up to you. You can implement some of the things you've learned right away. If there are things about you, or your marriage, that need to be addressed, please begin that process. Perhaps you need outside assistance. That's okay. If you feel or see some of these things in your church, don't be afraid to address them. Just don't let these things slip by—they are silent killers in an unseen war. Your life and the lives of your loved ones are at stake. My hope and prayers go with you.

Epilogue

MR. STAKES AND
MRS. CALCULATIONS

I loved my father-in-law who used to jokingly refer to psychologists as "those people who get paid to stick their noses in other people's business!" I concede now that he was right. I felt a definite burden from the Lord to write this book and to address these issues, but I shudder when I think about groups of power partners jumping out from behind bushes at me and shouting, "Why'd you have to go and write about this? Why couldn't you just leave well enough alone?" Or I tremble at the thought of an enraged passive partner coming at me in a dark alley and yelling, "What took you so long to get this information to me? I'm mad at my spouse and at you, too! Thanks for the ammunition. Now I'm loading up and firing at my spouse." (I assure you my intention was merely to point out that we, as Christians, can become blindly frozen in a mine field, rationalizing and telling ourselves that all is well when it is not. My intention was to remove the blindfold and guide you to safety.)

I felt the same way a number of years ago when I first read Bridges's *Pursuit of Holiness*. Ignorance was indeed bliss, and truth was painfully confronting. Once we've been exposed to the truth, however, the only choice left is whether or not we become obedient. In this case, obedience may necessitate patience in the midst of exasperation or require tolerance in the midst of awareness of the need for change.

I also anticipate reactions from power-passive leaders who fear being exposed (to others and/or themselves). Proficient power defenders worth their salt are adept at finding some point(s) of contention or disagreement and thereby feeling justified in rejecting all of the message of this book (e.g., "liberal," "secular," "unbiblical," etc.). Please don't buy that!

It is also a mistaken notion that this book worsens relationships or causes problems. It merely exposes what is already there but has not been recognized or acknowledged. All truth brings hidden issues, dynamics, or processes into the light.

The Danger of Impetuous Reaction

For many people, the contents of this book alone will be sufficient to bring about cooperative change. For other people, support groups will enhance and enliven the challenges presented. Yet for one other group of people, there will be an intense reaction that may lead to premature demands, unleased agitation, and impetuous actions.

This book has the tendency to turn on inner lights, to stir up feelings, and to generate energies seeking responsive action. My prayer is that such an energized awakening will take you to Christ rather than cause you to act out on those feelings in such a way that poses potential harm to you, your mate, or other loved ones. It is my further hope that what you learn about yourself and your situation will be used constructively as building blocks to the new you and the new relationship that Christ wants to establish. Much material has been outlined that can lead to individual and relational healing. I sincerely believe that Christ will heal every life and every relationship, no matter how severe, that is yielded to Him and is willing to stick to good biblical guidance and counseling as described in this book. For many people, most, if not all, of this work can be done within the local church. For another group of people, part(s), or all, may require professional help.

A Warning to the Passive Partner

If the power-passive relationship has dragged on long enough or penetrated deep enough, you may be like a Scud missile that has been readied for launching a megawarhead on it. *Stop! Don't fire!*

A common, albeit wrong, reaction is for passive partners to become so enraged or frustrated with their mates that they fire their missiles point-blank. Such an attack can come in the form of angry comments and behaviors, depression, anxiety, fear, abandonment of plans for counseling (or termination of existing counseling), and/or demands for immediate separation or divorce. There can also be a rally cry under the guise of Christian assertiveness that crosses over into non-Christian aggressiveness. *None* of these alternatives is biblically appropriate, though all of them are predictably understandable. Each of these reactions may worsen the overall individual and relational situation.

Your goal is obedience to Christ.

Stick with the game plan as outlined in this book. Don't make hasty decisions. Remember that you still see the world in a deceptive way. In such stressful times, you develop tunnel vision; you see only a limited number of options when there are a host of positive options available. Remember also that your immediate goal is obedience to Christ regardless of your immediate felt-needs. You are to never put the pursuit of holiness on hold. That response is disobedience. God can't honor disobedience, but He is waiting to pour out His healing and blessings upon those who practice complete submission to Him and to His will. Your situation with your spouse is first, and foremost, a situation with you and Christ.

A Caution to the Power Partner

Impulsiveness and impatience work both ways. Just as there will be a small number of passive partners who become disturbingly provoked, there will be a small number of power partners who become procedurally frustrated. These folks sound something like this: "What's wrong with my spouse now? I've read the book and made the changes. Why doesn't my spouse respond?" *Don't push!* Stick with the game plan. Any expectation of immediate and/or complete trust, forgive-and-forgetfulness, or business as usual becomes another type of abuse. It also feels like manipulativeness or control to your mate. Back off! Give your mate time. Give yourself time. Give your relationship time. The changes addressed in this book require changes in life-style—not just temporary patchwork. Pursue Christ. Your situation with your spouse is first, and foremost, a situation with you and Christ.

Establishment of Trust

A major task to work on during this period of relational healing is the development of new levels of trust: faith in the awareness you've gained from the material contained in this book; faith in Christ's ability to help you grow during and through this situation; faith in obedience to Christ and His will; faith in the knowledge that what He is working in you, and your mate, is a good thing; faith in your willingness to give to your mate and to take risks by becoming vulnerable to each other; and faith in your mate's commitment to following Christ and allowing Him to effect the individual and relational healing in His way, in His time.

Alarmed for the Alarmists

Just as there are power relationships, there are rigid mind-sets in the broad field of psychology and in the church. Such mentalities should be kept in perspective by the individual(s) trying to break away from these same processes as described in this book. Some extremes-oriented folks believe that any amount of psychology makes any approach using psychology all wrong. Remember that extremes-oriented thinking sees the world as black or white, right or wrong. "Psychology" is painted as the evil twin of the "correct" approach to counseling (that approach being largely dependent on who is addressing the issue). Some well-meaning approaches operationally and functionally plagiarize (I would hope unintentionally) psychological teachings, calling these psychological principles and processes something else that they have discovered (with scriptural support), then turning around and in the same breath attacking psychology as being wrong.

The term *psychology* has taken on new depth in the church and ministry of power partners. It has become a popular and easy task for rigid alarmists to bash psychology. Bully-bashers can appear quite intimidating, authoritative, puristic, and "spiritual" as they manhandle another of a string of ungodly foes that needs to be exposed to their helpless, naive, weak, immature, nonthinking, incompetent, and defenseless followers. All the while, they avoid responsibility for their own real psychological and spiritual problems and for the destruction and pain all around them that they cannot see or adequately understand. After all, how can they, or anyone, have psychological problems when, according to them, there isn't such a thing or when all psychology is automatically incorrect?

But what is *psychology*—this monster and threat to rigidity, passivity, and godliness? This book has endeavored to point out psychological blind spots and barriers to godliness—the rightful role of Christian psychology. The legitimate function of Christian counseling is to identify, expose, and overcome all psychological obstacles to holiness in an integrated way. The triune model necessitates the integration of theology (knowledge of God), psychology (understanding of a tainted self in a fallen world), consequential relationships (relationship to others), and their interconnectedness and ongoing union. The term *psychology* (or literally the study of the psyche or soul) is somewhat misleading in that we really need to think in terms of *psychologies*—the variety of approaches for studying and understanding human behavior and the mind. Anything that involves studying or trying to understand behavior or thought processes is definitionally, operationally, and de facto psychological. The term *Christian psychology* broadly means applying this same psychological endeavor to the Christian realm (but more specifically and accurately applies to those Christians trained in both psychology and Christian theology). This broader understanding, however, means that whenever anyone meets with a Christian for any kind of counseling, it is Christian counseling or a form of Christian psychology.

Psychology and *Christian psychology* are very broad terms that can be compared to the broad term *church*. There are misguided churches, ineffective pastors and leaders, and dangerous cults under the broad banner of the term *church*, but you don't decry, destroy, or reject the term or concept of *church* unless you're an adversary, misinformed, or a secular alarmist. Similarly, there are bad mental health facilities, bad practitioners and leaders, and all kinds of offshoots under the broad banner of the term *psychology*, but you don't decry, destroy, or reject the term or concept of *psychology*—especially *Christian psychology*—unless you're an adversary, misinformed, or a Christian alarmist. If you're a Christian, you automatically have Christian psychology in your life—psychological processes that affect or influence the Christian. This impact can range from various advertisements trying to persuade your thinking to the power partner trying to persuade your life.

Because psychology is so broad, it is easy prey for anyone who would try to discredit it. Surprisingly, and perhaps hypocritically, such attacks are almost always done by individuals who knowingly or unknowingly use some form of psychology anyway. They may call it something else or try to spiritualize their approach, but if it looks like a duck . . . by golly, it's a duck! So then it's not a matter of whether or not psychology is legitimate or operable (it is); it's a matter of how well the individual(s) honestly and competently understand these very processes, mechanisms, and dynamics, intellectually and personally.

A favorite way to attack psychology is to use a variety of straw man arguments usually related to some far-out area of psychology and then turn around and say that all psychologists—even Christian psychologists—believe these bizarre teachings. It's just not true. People tend to believe gossip and unthinkingly accept whatever is told them instead of more fully investigating allegations. No wonder those grocery store newspapers thrive so well—people want to listen to the outrageous. It would be just as logical to attack the church by stating that all churches are misleading people because a representative church, cult, or church leader did so (the press can provide a long list of suspect individuals, and usually does).

Poor Freud. He's a favorite for such straw man arguments, yet I don't know any psychologists—especially Christian psychologists or counselors—who believe all that Freud taught. Christian counselors who seek to integrate their approach will find components from his teaching useful (such as unconscious processes) but will automatically reject everything that is unbiblical. Yet they are portrayed by alarmists as buying everything hook, line, and sinker! That simply isn't true. Admittedly, some psychologists out there use New Age teachings. But there are also Christian psychologists and counselors who are aware of these things and appropriately integrate psychology and Christian theology.

These same alarmists turn right around and use and/or teach their "correct" approach to counseling (remember that all counseling is psychological) while assailing other (psychological) approaches that differ from their own (despite their limited training and understanding in the area), proclaiming all psychology to be something automatically ungodly. Certainly, there is a lot within the broad field of psychology to question, and there are definite areas to reject. But this same kind of reasoning also means that if one pastor, one church leader, or one church does something considered to be unbiblical or wrong, all church is bad. I'm sometimes amazed and frightened by what such alarmists say that I, and other Christians who attempt to integrate Christianity and psychology, actually believe.

I often wish that some of the misguided energies by power-oriented critics could be used to come alongside us at the front lines of wounded individuals' psychological and spiritual battles—or to explain some of their own assorted but questionable stances concerning such issues as the denial of the supernatural, the lack of understanding of unconscious processes, the ignorance or denial of spiritual warfare in counseling, the lack of clinical experiences and training, personal woundedness, or power issues, etc., rather than blaming or attacking psychology for things not fully understood, experienced, or appreciated.

But let's not get bogged down in wishful thinking, semantics, power games, or power struggles. Jesus is Lord of all—even of psychology. Secular counselors may not recognize that fact, but that doesn't make it any less true. The variety of Christian counselors may not adequately recognize and appreciate that Jesus is Lord of all our forms of psychology (just as He is Lord of all denominations within Christianity).

I hope you can get an idea of this maze of deceptive confusion and boldly pursue assistance from a well-respected helper who is also highly credentialed, skilled, and well-trained in both the field of theology and the field of psychology. The person's counseling approach should be based on the lordship of Christ and the authority of Scripture, supplemented by skilled application of psychological principles, techniques, and processes. Don't be scared away, confused, or intimidated by those who just don't understand or who fight because of their own psychological baggage. The issues addressed in this book represent the integration of the psychological and spiritual realms. Don't wimp out!

Confusion Leads to Emotional and Spiritual Diffusion and Disunity

The effects of all these attacks on one another by varied counseling theorists—especially attacks waged at the correct Christian psychology—tend to scare Christians away from all kinds of counseling and legitimate help. The result is confusion and lack of help, or partial help based on partial understanding and partial truth, which leads to emotional and spiritual disunity of the affected individuals and the church.

We Christians need to quit the game playing, name-calling, and blackballing that we do with one another to decide whose psychology is correct. We should be ashamed and embarrassed about how we speak so demeaningly of one another and one another's views of Christian counseling. Just as members of different denominations can come together at a higher level in Christ, the various Christian counseling approaches should work harder at loving one another and at seeking unity at least at the level of our spiritual oneness.

Don't be dissuaded. Psychology is a gift from God. It is a part of general revelation. General revelation is just as true and valid as special revelation. What we do with psychology is something else. A scalpel in the hand of a competent, caring, qualified surgeon can complement God's healing process. A switchblade on the street is potentially harmful and deadly. Similarly, psychology in the hands of a competent, caring, qualified caregiver (e.g., psychologist, counselor, physician, pastor, spouse, church member, etc.) can complement God's healing process. Misused psychology is potentially harmful. Beware of approaches that stir up dissension and disunity among believers. Beware of approaches that are rigid. Look for balance. Look for honesty and integrity. Look for competence. Look for truth. Look for healing. Look for Christ.

Courage in the Church

It will take courage to address the power-passive dynamics in the church. Obviously, it should be done in love, with prayer, and in consideration of the weaker members. Healthy brothers or sisters are willing to examine themselves in these areas. Unhealthy sisters or brothers will become defensive and resistive. Such persons may feel threatened, offended, or attacked, and they may lead an attack against you or try to discredit your message. Your situation in your church is first, and foremost, a situation with you and Christ. Ask Him to lead you and to use you if your particular situation calls for someone to stand up for His will there. Remember that all forms of control, rigidity, and passivity are unbiblical, and they can become silent destroyers of ministries of the church.

Overcoming the Enemy

I certainly want to close with words of encouragement. I hope that the contents of this book have challenged you to a recognition of an insidious and deceptive threat to the sanctity of marriage and to the purity of the church.

With Christ, there is victory. There is no enemy too strong; no plot, scheme, or psychological mechanism too deceptive; no adversary too pervasive that Christ has not already won the war. Our hope is not in ourselves; it is in Him. He loves you; He cares about your situation; He will deliver you if you'll let Him. Commit all of the things you've learned about yourself, your mate, your relationship, and your church to the Lord Jesus Christ. Commit yourself, your mate, your family, and your problems to Him. Victory awaits—in Him.